The Heart of America

A World War II veteran celebrates Memorial Day in New York City.

Kevin Fleming

ISBN 0-9662423-7-8 • ©MMIV • All rights reserved

Pope John Paul II, Washington, D.C.

Delaware firefighters

Migrant worker camp, Delaware

Chasing the Light

Triumphs, tragedies, natural disasters – you name it – whatever made the front page was my assignment.

I loved the challenge and excitement of news photography and I loved the "rush" I got from capturing a decisive moment on film and then seeing the image in the newspaper the next day.

As the years passed, however, I wanted to explore the world and photograph faraway places. So I left Delaware newspaper deadlines behind and spent a decade circling the globe as a *National Geographic* photographer. Assignments included everything from daily life near the North Pole to re-creating the Bronze Age voyage of Ulysses to scientific experiments at high-energy physics labs.

I was also fascinated by the challenge of magazine feature photography – the struggle to catch that single moment when light and shape and color combine to form an unforgettable image.

Still, I never quite lost my "nose for news," as the daily journalists like to call it. While on assignment in war-torn Somalia and Ethiopia, I held on and held my breath as I drove an old Land Rover as fast as possible along deeply rutted desert roads laced with deadly land mines. If I drove fast enough, the mines would explode behind me.

Dispatched to Egypt by *National Geographic* for a feature story on the Sinai Peninsula, I was with President Anwar Sadat when he was assassinated in cold blood. While grenades exploded and machine guns fired all around me, I somehow managed to capture that tragic moment on film.

Maybe it was this combination of news and feature journalism that eventually got me interested in creating books of photographs. Here was a format that could bring together a hundred or more images to tell a story. Before **The Heart of America**, I authored 13 photography books, mostly regional titles.

Now a book about America started taking shape. Some of the photographs here are from *National Geographic* and other magazine assignments. A few are from my previous books. With generous support from Corbis, the stock photography agency owned by Microsoft founder Bill Gates, and friend and sponsor Alex Pires, I began traveling across the country as often as possible. On September 11, 2001, when I saw the second airplane crash into the World Trade Center, I realized that America – and the world – were changed forever. That day, I changed too. A sense of urgency compelled me to get back on the road and finish this book.

But what is America? Is there a way to understand it? Are there any links, any connections that could somehow tie together people and cultures so vastly different? Is there a "hidden connection" that might reveal the deep-down similarities between cattle ranchers in West Texas and lobstermen in Maine?

Like Charles Kuralt, the great CBS television newsman whose "On The Road" series captured so many unforgettable American landscapes and personalities, I packed my camera gear and a few supplies and traveled back and forth across America in search of people and places and stories.

By helicopter and hot-air balloon. . . by kayak and snowshoe and river raft and horseback, I found hundreds of fascinating Americans and their equally fascinating stories. I spent as much time as possible in each and every one of the 50 states.

During my odyssey, I learned America is a vast, sweeping landscape where climates and vistas and people and cultures vary so widely – and so frequently – that it's almost impossible to make generalities about the "heart" of this great country.

But I managed to identify a few common threads. I found the people – regardless of educational levels and regardless of ethnic backgrounds – to be extraordinarily hospitable, helpful and friendly. In situation after situation, I was amazed, even shocked, by the generosity and kindness of the folks I met and photographed. In rural Arkansas, I spent a couple of days with a family whose house had no indoor plumbing. Their life seemed a struggle, yet these kind people welcomed me into their lives and insisted I stay with them as long as possible.

It was the same story almost everywhere I went. In Philadelphia, mobs of brightly painted and colorfully dressed "Mummers" not only allowed me to photograph their parade – they wanted me to march with them from beginning to end. At a major NASCAR race, the officials were so helpful they actually put me in the pace car for the start of a 400-lap event. A Hutterite farm commune in North Dakota not only fed and sheltered their visiting photographer – they even "allowed" me to work beside them for a day harvesting potatoes.

It was always the same. I journeyed from state to state, mostly avoiding the major highways in favor of the countryside and smaller towns. I found myself visiting with the Amish at a farm auction in Delaware, riding on horseback along-side working cowboys on cattle ranches in Wyoming, and sharing the solitude of a Navajo medicine man in the New Mexico desert.

I hope you'll see in these photographs that the American people are unrivaled in their generosity with strangers, and for their enthusiastic willingness to share their worlds with respectful outsiders curious about their ways of life.

Another thread I discovered was the way ordinary sunlight – especially at dawn and dusk – brings its own special chemistry to every setting. Again and again, I used light as the verb in my photographs and allowed its color, strength and intensity to reveal and illuminate my subjects. Without using a single filter or any artificial source of lighting, I captured these photographs for **The Heart of America**, letting the people be themselves and the light paint the landscapes.

Kevin Fleming

Civil War in Ethiopia

Sadat assasination, Egypt

Famine in Somalia

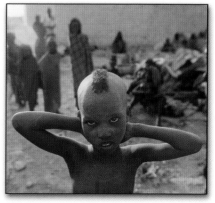

African refugees

Meet Jeremy Hobbs, "Opie" to his friends. You'll find his family's "You-Pick-'Em" strawberry patch near Viola, Delaware (left).

Jennifer Hobbs, Jeremy's mom, has a high opinion of his skills as a harvester of the plump red fruit: "That boy can pick a pretty good quart of berries!"

I began my journey across America here, on Jeremy's one-acre berry patch. I wanted to start at dawn in the height of spring, standing where I could feel the earth through the soles of my feet.

I grew up here, in rural Delaware, just up the road from Jeremy's farm. As a youngster, I plowed and planted this land. In the summertime I muscled hay bales into the barn and sweated in the 100-degree heat.

I picked a few strawberries, too.

But that was 35 years ago. Look at the yellow sunrise blossoming behind Jeremy's shoulder. It won't last too long. Just time enough for a photograph and then I'll move on.
Look at the ripe fruit heaped in his baskets. Any wonder Jeremy is smiling?

A few miles to the south, near Felton, I ran into a man (following pages) dedicated to keeping history alive. Bill Paskey – a fifth-generation grain farmer and tavern operator – astonished his neighbors a few years ago. In his yard, he restored a 19th-century farmhouse and added an old one-room school. Next came antique tractors and a railroad complete with a retired locomotive, cars, caboose and train station, plus three acres full of ancient farm equipment. Old Glory hangs from the grain elevator he uses to store his crops.

Looking around his homespun museum, I realized Bill is determined to hold onto the past.

That's six-year-old Taylor Lynn holding on to her daddy's neck. She doesn't want to let go, either.

Do they love their old cars in Beaver Falls, Pennsylvania, or what? These two excited boys jumped into a vintage 1960 Lincoln Continental for a ride along the main street of town. I watched the spontaneous parade of antique autos snake through the downtown intersection, then lurch off toward the concrete bridge that spans the muddy Beaver River.

At seven degrees above zero, the North Atlantic spray freezes your eyebrows and spikes your hair. The lobstermen of Monhegan Island – a hunk of wind-scoured granite perched 10 miles off the Maine seacoast – fish throughout the months of January and February, under conditions so brutal they leave no room for mistakes.

Piloting sturdy workboats like the Casey Anne (previous pages) through 50-mile-an-hour gales, these risk-defying lobstermen work long hours for uncertain pay. Will the next trap they haul to the surface be empty or full?

I thought I'd been cold during two previous assignments near the North Pole. But this deep-freeze felt different. Maybe it was the wind driving the sea spray into the back of my neck. Or maybe it was the silence. These lobstermen don't talk much. What is there to say? In the winter they inhabit a world so cold that an accident means almost certain death.

Today lobster fishermen often use high-tech satellite navigation to find their pots, and feather-light Styrofoam buoys (following pages) that cannot mangle their propellers during collisions at the top of a wave.

But there's no high-tech solution for winter storms, and each haul of a lobster trap is still a roll of the dice. These mariners are strong and resourceful and plenty smart; why don't they seek easier, better-paying jobs ashore? Why do they return generation after generation to their storm-wracked ocean?

Lobsterman Skeet MacDonald (right) chased the elusive delicacy around his Maine islands until finally retiring at the tender age of 93. He worked hard, yet he also knew how to laugh. When I asked him to show me his traps, the resident of Isle au Haut was happy to oblige. "These are my poverty crates!" he said with a lighthearted chuckle. A minute later, he was hauling an armload of battered pots toward his waiting boat.

New England junk dealer Bill Buckminister (left) scratches out a precarious living by salvaging and then peddling relics of the past in Owls Head, Maine. He spotted that jumbo-sized lobster during a local seafood festival parade. Bill gets by on the strength of his wits, along with lots of Yankee ingenuity. Unable to support a full-time junkyard dog, he makes do with a picture of a mean one.

A few miles down the road, I wandered into a scrap yard that had become an unofficial museum for ancient

American cars. Closed more than 40 years ago, the weed-laced junkyard was crammed with World War II-vintage Studebakers and LaSalles. This rusting auto hulk (above) – a late-1930s Packard – serves as a fascinating time capsule from FDR's second term.

As a photographer, I make an awful lot of U-turns – and I always brake for roadside giraffes. This one (following pages) materialized at an outdoor antiques emporium in Bethlehem, New Hampshire.

At Mystic, Connecticut, the famed Seaport Museum (previous pages) slumbered through a chill, windless dawn. In an age when tall ships ruled the seas and clipper ships were the fastest way to circle the globe, Mystic's famous wooden boat-building shipyards buzzed with activity. Today, North America's largest maritime museum welcomes visitors from around the world – so it's still a very busy place. Light is a verb, it often seems to me… and the action at Mystic was just beginning on this cold winter morning.

After another snowstorm, I rented a Piper Cub airplane at Manchester, New Hampshire, and found a series of towns so quintessentially "New England" that they reminded me of Currier & Ives lithographs of the mid-1800s. This village (left) has barely changed its appearance in the past hundred years. The light held it up to me for a moment, and I did my best to "write it down" with a camera.

In Washington, New Hampshire, the first American town to be named after the first American president, I saw four kids dragging a Christmas tree home. It was late afternoon by now (following pages), and the last of the twilight bathed the church spire, town hall and school in a soft amber glow. And it seemed as if time had been frozen in these corners of New England.

23

Not a creature was stirring on that snowy afternoon in Warwick, Rhode Island – so there was no way to tell if these stockings had been "hung with care" (previous pages). I hit the brakes hard and slid to a stop to see this inside-out Christmas display.

Atop Cadillac Mountain in Maine's Acadia National Park, cross-country skiers skimmed the surface of what looked like the next Great Ice Age (left). The park draws more than a million visitors each summer – but then the trails freeze over and the roads become choked with snow. Drop by in January and the only sound you'll hear is the wind gnawing at trees capped with ice.

Farther south, near Gap, Pennsylvania, Tim Jobe, winemaker and general manager of Twin Brook Winery (following pages), feels that same winter chill as he makes his rounds inspecting recently pruned vines.

At the dawn of the 20th century during America's Gilded Age, the Rockefellers, Vanderbilts, Biltmores and the Mellons lived in dazzling summer homes and Newport, Rhode Island (previous pages) was the playground of the nation's rich and famous. Today, dozens of French-style châteaus, Victorian and Italian Renaissance -style villas and Tudor palaces line the waterfront, with many under the care of the Preservation Society of Newport County and open for public tours.

I found this particular palace from a helicopter as the sunrise crawled with fog, and the pale mist went through my rotor blades like wisps of cotton candy.

If the white tabby (left) looks smug and self-satisfied, it's probably because he lives in a brick mansion on Boston's super-exclusive Beacon Hill.

I was feeling a bit smug myself, as I ambled along the cobblestones and imagined I was retracing the footsteps of some of America's Founding Fathers. Surely Sam Adams, Paul Revere and their Revolutionary pals had lived and worked in this pricey neighborhood, way back in 1776.

Wrong. As I later discovered at the venerable Boston Public Library, Beacon Hill hadn't been developed until the early 1800s. For Adams & Co., it was just a pasture on the outskirts of town! Oh, well. I still like the cat in the window.

Near Andersonville, Georgia, about 50 miles north of Atlanta, I saw a boy playing in a creek. He was there for the town's annual Spring Fair, a festival featuring Civil War battle reenactments, historically authentic encampments and even a blacksmith. Pausing for a moment under the old wooden footbridge, he looked into my camera. I felt like I was looking back in time too.

Up the coast, in the heart of the low country, quaint old Charleston, South Carolina, is a treasure trove of antebellum architecture. In block after block, one house after another has been restored to pre-Civil War grandeur. True to the city's old-fashioned appearance, even the classic neon advertising of Tellis Pharmacy seems historic.

Caught in the gentle glow of a Delaware dawn, this granite water tower (left) on a sprawling duPont estate – Granogue – mimics a medieval lookout or a fairy-tale prison cell for Rapunzel.

But the structure actually serves a more utilitarian purpose as the reservoir for one of America's most beautiful country estates. Built from elegant Germantown stone in the early 1920s by industrial magnate Irénée duPont, the nearby mansion features 11 sumptuous bedrooms and 515 acres of fields and rolling woodland. Says Granogue's current occupant, Irénée duPont Jr.: "It's going to be the devil's own job to tear it down – but not on my watch."

The mighty Chesapeake Bay Bridge soars 399 feet in the air and crosses more than four miles of open water. Twenty million vehicles cross the twin spans each year. Impressive? You bet. But more memorable for me was the tranquility of this moment as a sloop motored down Maryland's Whitehall Creek for a sail on the bay. Here the engineering marvel seems dwarfed by the vastness of the estuarine landscape.

Have you been lucky enough to taste a
blue crab – the delightful East Coast delicacy
that's steamed with a sprinkling of Old
Bay seasoning, then hammered open and
picked apart? Ever wonder how they
catch 'em? Most commercial watermen
put out hundreds of fish-baited wire crab
traps in brackish water and shallow tidal
marshes along the coast. Then they
return the next day to shake out their
catch and rebait their pots.

There's another way to catch crabs,
however. The way lifelong Chesapeake
Bay waterman Gordon Kolsox (right)
does it. His simple approach requires little
more than a boat and a rope. Gordon
baits a "trotline" with pieces of salted eel
or chicken necks. Secured by buoys at
both ends, the rope rests on the bottom
long enough to attract crabs. He draws
the rope over a roller as the boat glides
forward. The crabs hold on until the last
second… and that's when Gordon deftly
nets them. One at a time.

Wind and waves, tide and twilight color
a rocky beach on Martha's Vineyard
(following pages) in Massachusetts.

Maine innkeeper Jim Rutland swoops low over Penobscot Bay in his home-built "Longeasy" airplane at 180 mph, cutting almost three hours from his car commute to Boston. There he climbs aboard a much larger plane – a Delta Airlines jumbo passenger jet – and puts in his next shift as a commercial pilot.

Just a mile from Philadelphia's Center City, with six lanes of expressway traffic roaring behind me, I came across a man (following pages) who'd somehow managed to find himself an unlikely patch of solitude on the Schuylkill River.

To photograph New York City's Chrysler Building – the world's tallest skyscraper in 1930 (below), and the Brooklyn Bridge – the world's first steel suspension bridge in 1883 (right), I relied on a most precarious perch – a tiny R-22 helicopter, one of the world's smallest.

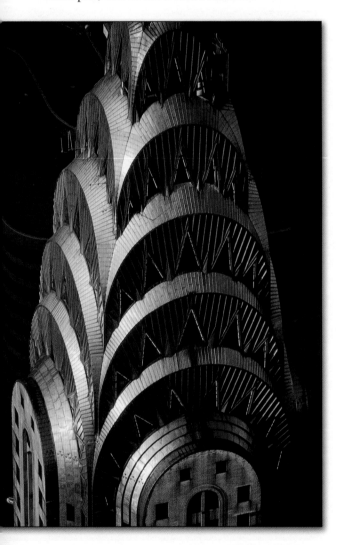

The helicopter was so cramped with cameras, lenses and film that I had to remove the door and lean out. At times it felt like I was as much outside as in. I remember a special freedom in the air that day. Flying up Fifth Avenue below the skyline and so close to New York's landmarks just isn't allowed by the government anymore. Not since September 11, 2001.

Before and after the tragedy: What can I say about the unspeakable horror of September 11th that hasn't already been said? I prefer to think of happier days. . . such as this Memorial Day celebration on Manhattan's Lower East Side (left). How

uncanny it now seems – the way a burst of aerial rockets momentarily formed a heart in the twilight sky. Two years after the World Trade Center attack, more somber memorial lights reach silently toward the heavens (above).

If there's a more instantly recognizable symbol of America in the 21st century, I've yet to hear about it. Since it was erected in New York Harbor in 1886, the 151-foot-high steel, bronze and copper sculpture (right) has become a worldwide icon of America.

It happens every November – the 26-mile-long bout of madness known as the New York City Marathon (below). The race begins on Staten Island, typically with more than 25,000 runners waiting impatiently for the blast of a howitzer cannon that signals the start of the action.

Winded competitors stream across the Verrazano Narrows Bridge, then pound the pavements of all five New York City boroughs. . . with some of them requiring five, six, even eight hours or more to reach the finish line.

The NYC Marathon isn't the nation's largest – that honor goes to San Francisco – and it isn't the oldest – Boston hosted America's first 26-miler way back in 1897 – but it's the only one you can run by subway, if you prefer. And that's exactly how I managed to shoot both the start of the race and the winner crossing the finish line!

Founded by legendary American painter Charles Willson Peale in 1805, the venerable Pennsylvania Academy of the Fine Arts (right) has long reigned as the crown jewel of Philadelphia's Center City art district. America's oldest fine arts school continues to insist on a studio-based "Old Masters" method for teaching painting, sculpture and printmaking. Although the school's rigorous courses in drawing and sculpting from "real life" attract enthusiastic artists from around the world, this mode of instruction can produce some challenging logistical problems.

Example: On the day I dropped by with my camera, I found a large horse posing calmly and patiently in a crowded second floor studio – after a nervous ride on an Academy freight elevator.

Rosemont College (above), an all-women's bastion of liberal arts located on Philadelphia's affluent Main Line since 1921, emphasizes both a sound mind and a healthy body for its nearly 1,100 students.

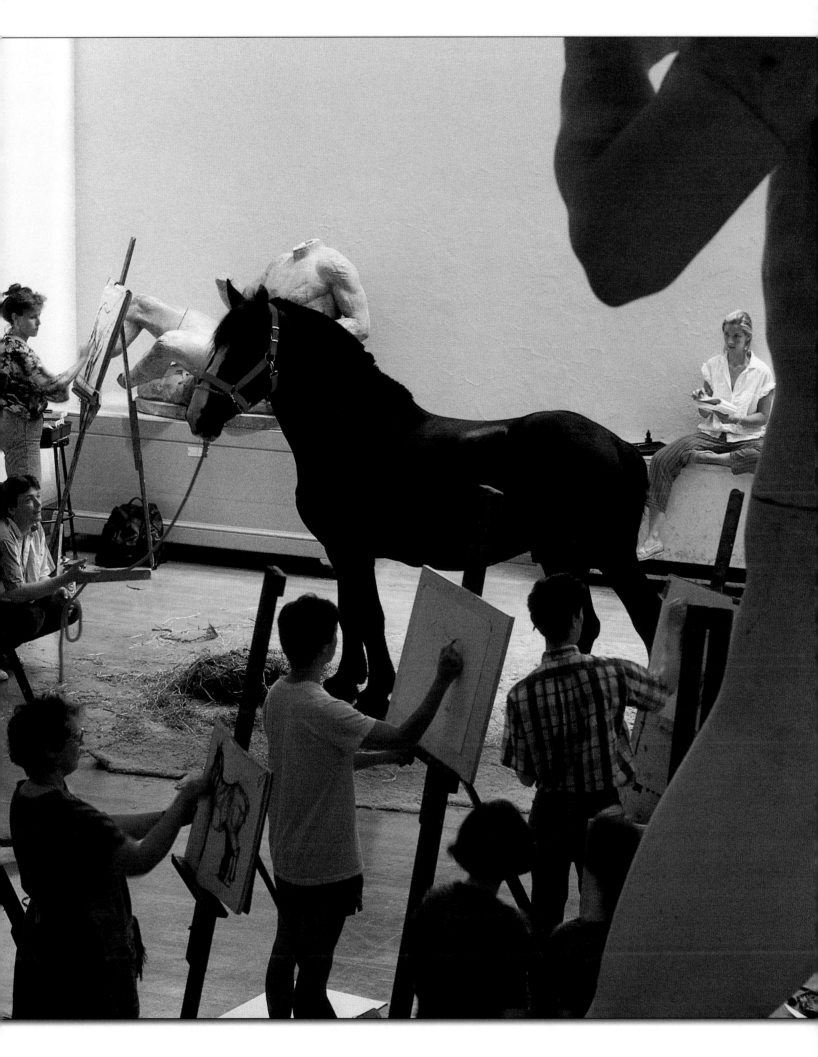

Wearing outlandish "Raggedy Andy" clown costumes and roaring with happy-hour euphoria, a mob of Mummers lurches toward Broad Street in downtown Philadelphia (previous pages). The annual Mummers Day Parade "strut" includes more than 15,000 performers. While some dress up in outrageously feathered and sequined costumes (the "Fancies") and others strum raucous banjos (the "String Bands"), many participants prefer to don clown paint and garish carnival garb (the "Comics") for a wildly intoxicating march through the city. Watching this crowd of parasol-waggling Comics cavort past a half-million cheering fans, I kept remembering Albert Einstein's wonderful remark: "Reality is not only stranger than we imagine – it's stranger than we can imagine!"

(Ditto for Philadelphia, at least on New Year's Day.)

Once restricted to white males, the Mummers Day extravaganza now celebrates cultural diversity as evidenced by a traditional Asian dance group (left) that brought vivid colors and exotic pageantry to a recent New Year's celebration in the "City of Brotherly Love."

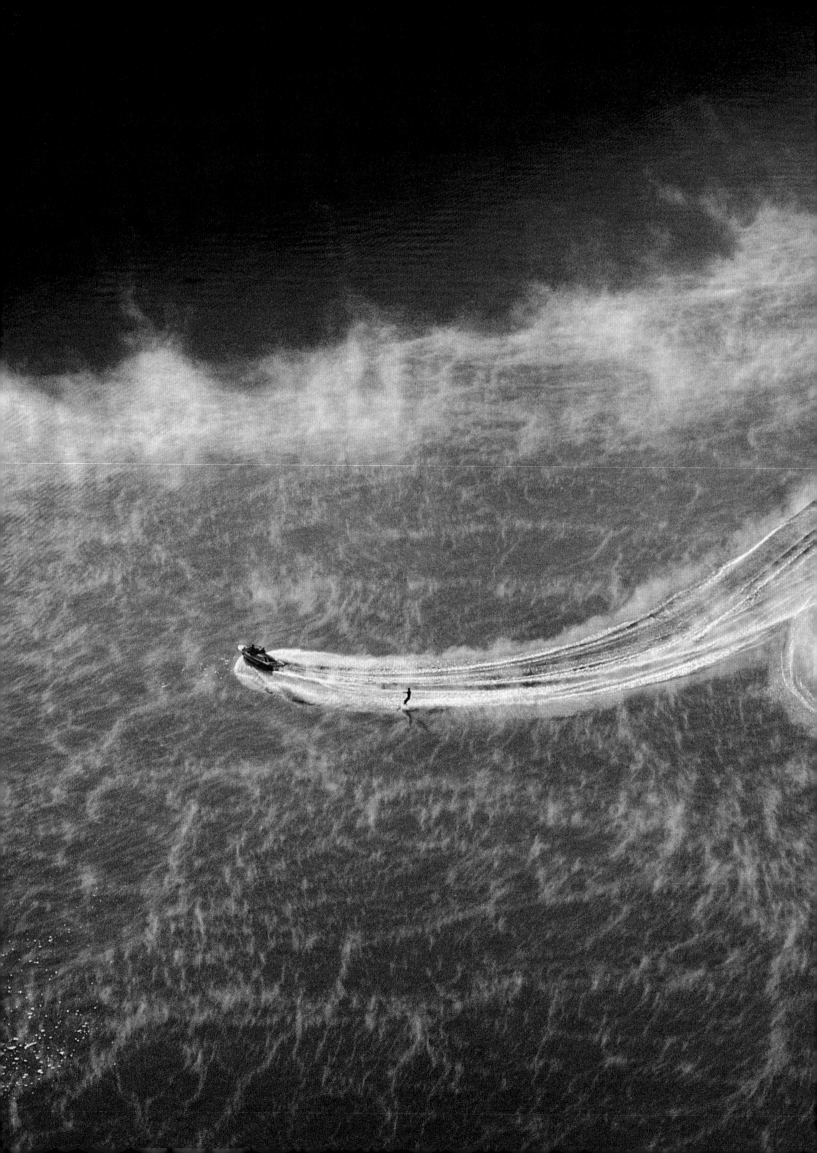

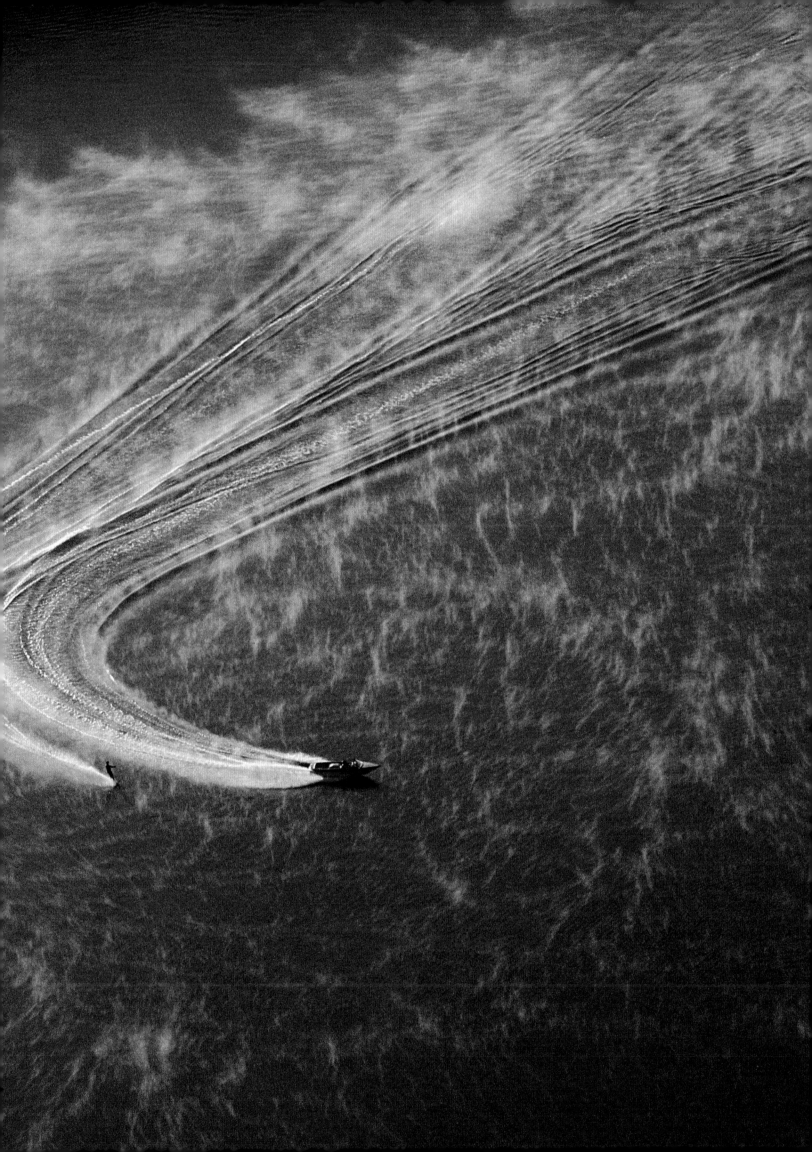

Leaning out of a helicopter, I raced to keep up with two water skiers twisting and turning along Maryland's South River (previous pages) on an October dawn. A tributary of the Chesapeake Bay, the brackish river was warmer than the surrounding air – producing swirls of pinkish mist that added splendor to the scene. There wasn't a breath of wind, and the surface was smooth as a mirror. I shot roll after roll of film as the pair carved graceful lines across the water with their skis.

The names here are not famous. Along America's Sunrise Coast, there's no Diamond Head, Waimea Bay or "Pipeline" as in Hawaii. But there can be some pretty spectacular surfing. (Depending on the weather, that is.) When an offshore hurricane churns the North Atlantic or a nor'easter howls past, surfers from Maine to Florida grab their boards and head for the beach. Here (left), Matt Naylor, better known as "Smiley," catches a ride at Delaware's Indian River Inlet. I'll bet he was smiling to the max on that ride.

Believe it or not, kids want to go to summer school in Ocean City, New Jersey. Already gung-ho wave riders, these avid youngsters (above) were headed toward a surfing class when I caught them crossing the boardwalk.

A Delaware "skimboarder" (left) catches the face of a wave near Dewey Beach. Unlike surfers, skimboarders run along the beach and toss their super-light foam boards onto the broken crest (or skim) of a wave. Rides usually last 10 seconds or less – the length of time it takes speeding water to reach the sand. Pros and amateurs compete every summer in Dewey Beach, home of the East Coast Skimboarding Championships.

"Go fetch" and "roll over" are tricks for any ordinary dog. This pooch (right) has gone way beyond the basics and is more into recreational water sports. I encountered the air-borne

"man and best friend" duo jumping boat wakes on Florida's Intracoastal Waterway near Fort Lauderdale.

Far from the ocean, Disney works its own aquatic magic, making four-foot waves every 90 seconds at its 2.75 million-gallon surf pool in "Typhoon Lagoon" near Orlando, Florida (above).

Placid and tranquil for much of its 383-mile run, the Potomac River explodes into dangerous whitewater as mountain-fed runoff crashes headlong into jagged granite at Great Falls, Maryland (previous pages). Here expert kayakers challenge themselves against nature, plunging 20 feet straight down on these "Class 5" rapids. Jason Robertson, who frequently dares this stretch of boiling turbulence, told me, "I live life to the fullest here."

There are few tougher rapids in all of America – and I was happy to catch this action from the sideline.

Roller coaster thrill-seekers (left) find plenty of wild rides on any of Cedar Point's 16 wooden and steel screamers. The Ohio amusement park claims the titles of the "World's Fastest" (120 mph) and the "World's Tallest" (420 feet) roller coasters.

Fewer than one in 10 of America's minor league baseball players will ever make it to "The Show" – the major leagues – where players often become celebrities and can earn more than a million dollars a season. For those who labor in the minors, such as former "Class A" Albany (Georgia) Polecats pitcher Chris Nygaard (blowing bubble, following pages), the daily grind includes endless fast-food joints, motel rooms and bus rides.

Why do they hang on year after year at the lower levels of America's most popular sport? Chris told me he didn't mind the bad food and the tedium. . . as long as he could chase his dream of someday "making the bigs." And his persistence paid off! Chris beat the long odds – and wound up pitching for the Montreal Expos in 2001.

Do Americans love pro football? The sport draws more than 16 million fans a year to stadiums across the country – with most happy to pay at least $40 for a ticket and up to $4 for a hot dog.

Philadelphia Eagles running back Brian Westbrook (below) carries the ball and an airborne San Francisco 49ers tackler downfield. An elusive running back, Westbrook averaged 5.2 yards per ramble during a recent season.

Lacrosse may be less well known and attended than football in America, but don't tell that to the thousands of players and fans who have made this rock 'em-sock 'em sport hugely popular all across New England and the Mid-Atlantic states during the past few decades. Taking an icy bath in this post-game celebration (left) was lacrosse coach John Coveleski of Caesar Rodney High School in Delaware after his hard-charging Riders had just won their third statewide title within a decade. John's instant analysis of the victory? "We were on fire!"

You don't watch a NASCAR race. You experience it. You feel the thunder of 43 high-performance race cars as they blur by. Every time the lead changes, the crowd roars and the jam-packed stands vibrate with excitement.

At Dover International Speedway in Delaware, 140,000 adoring fans (following pages) turn out twice a year to spend several hours cheering the race-car drivers they worship. And they aren't alone; recent marketing surveys show that fully half of America's 200 million adults will watch at least one NASCAR race (in person or televised) each year.

Out on the steeply banked concrete "Monster Mile," the brightly painted cars hurtle along at close to 200 mph, and a single miscalculation can instantly lead to disaster. And the action in the "pits" is just as fast and furious. Each second

here equals 100 yards out on the track, which explains why these finely tuned crews can change four tires, fill 22 gallons of gas and clean a driver's windshield in less than 15 ticks of a stopwatch. Any wonder that the Dale Earnhardt Jr. pit crew (right) seems almost airborne, as they fly through their paces on car number 8?

Hanging out of the "pace car" and balancing my backside on the window frame, I gripped a camera in one hand and held on for dear life with the other. NASCAR officials had promised me the pace laps before the start of the race wouldn't be faster than 40 mph.

Yeah, right. We hit 40 mph before the first turn. And way faster after that.

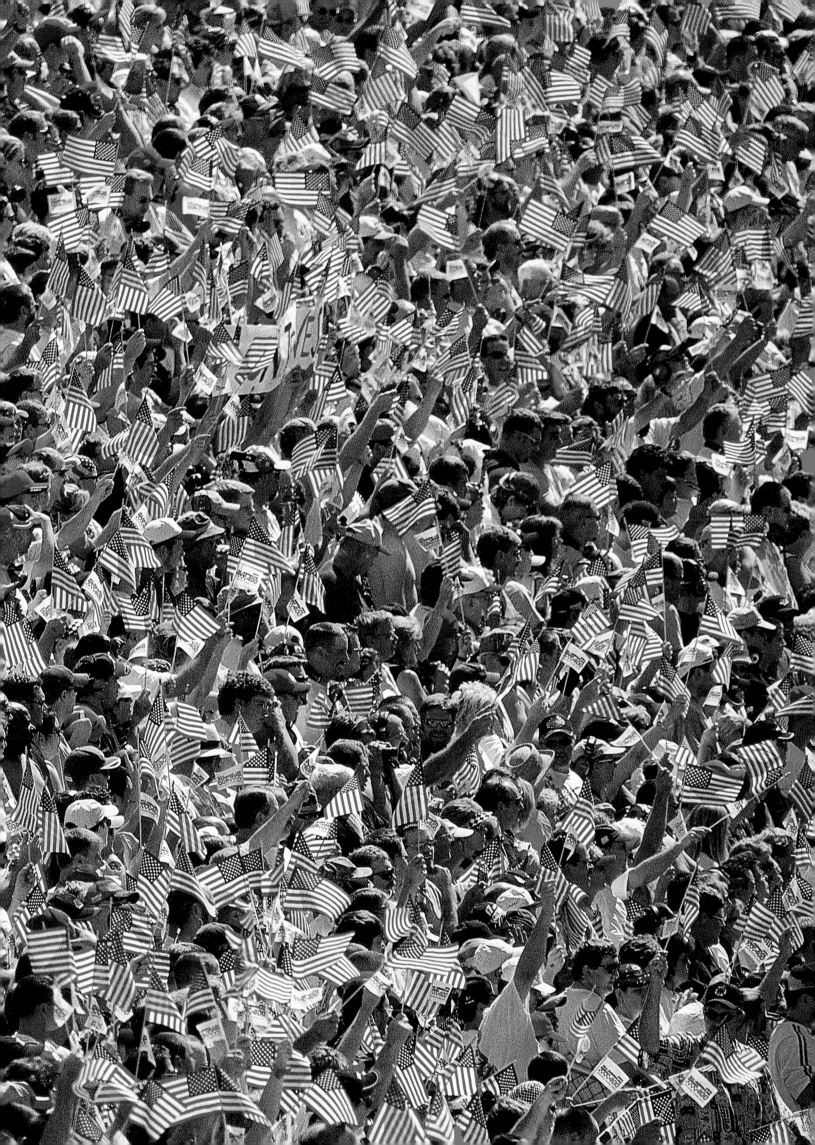

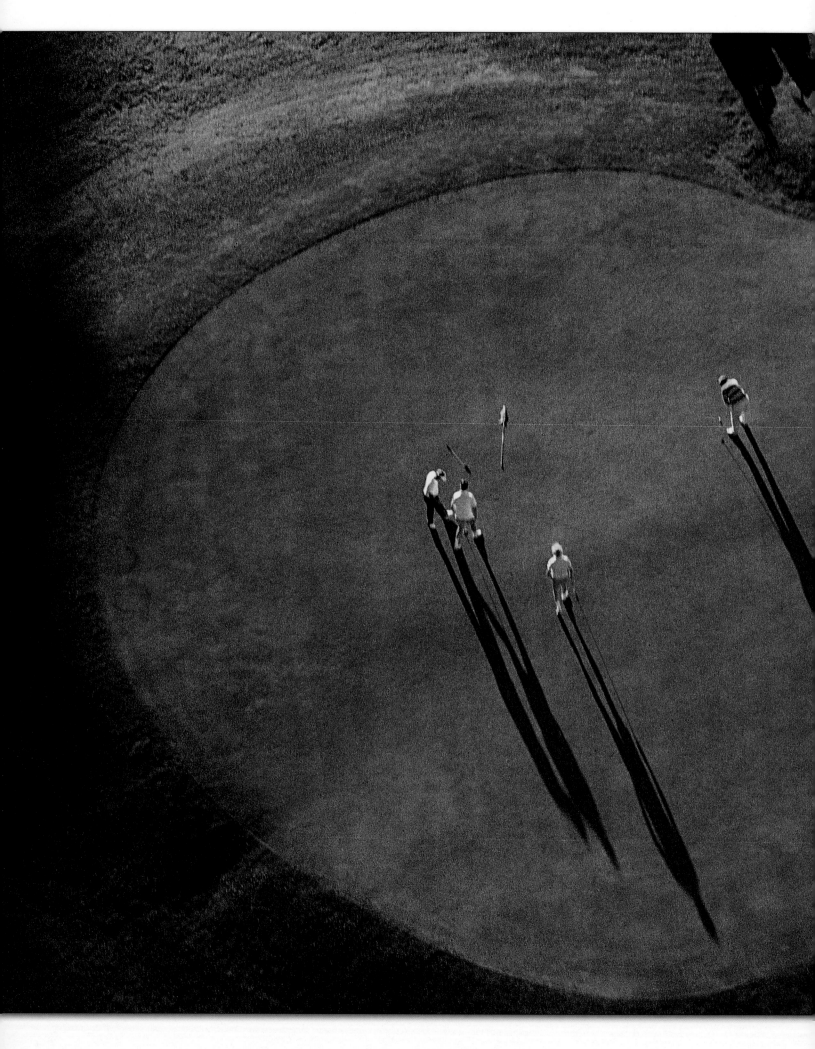

Mark Twain once described golf as "a good walk, spoiled" but many Americans would probably disagree with him. U.S. golfers approach the game with a passion that borders on obsession: 27 million play the links regularly and they spend upwards of $15 billion a year doing so.

This summertime action (left) was on the 16th hole at a country club course near Sandy Spring, Maryland.

The dawn was just breaking when I spotted a horse-trainer leading a mare and her prancing foal across a sun-gilded pasture near Chesapeake City, Maryland (previous pages). The Old Line State is a major player in the $25 billion-a-year U.S. horseracing industry, with numerous thoroughbred farms like this one competing for a shot at the fabled Kentucky Derby.

The competition is fierce, as you might imagine. Only a dozen or so thoroughbreds will qualify for the annual "Run for the Roses" – after two years of relentless training and grooming. Impeccable bloodlines and millions of dollars of horseracing expertise are required for success, but owners who make the starting gate at Churchill Downs also need lots of old-fashioned luck.

Betting everything on one camera under the railing at the finish line, I crossed my fingers as I watched the Kentucky Derby in Louisville. Called the "most exciting two minutes in sports," I wanted to be close enough to see the race from ground level, so I set up my camera just inches from the track. Horse hooves pounded by and the race was over in an instant. But I hadn't thought about the flying mud. One look at the smeared camera lens and I felt my heart sink. All I could do now was wait – I wouldn't know until I saw the film if the horses had beaten the mud to the finish line.

Thoroughbreds thunder to the finish line at Delaware Park in Stanton (left), home of the $500,000 Delaware Handicap. Opened in 1937 as one of the East Coast's major tracks for

June racing, the verdant 600-acre venue is known as one of the prettiest tracks in the nation.

Horsepower of another kind streaks toward the girls high school state track championship in Albany, Georgia (above).

Hide-and-seek becomes life and death for a lobster dodging a scuba diver (left) in the Elkhorn coral of Florida's Biscayne Bay. It was the first day of lobster season and the skittish crustaceans were doing their best to make themselves scarce.

Viewed from the air, dive boats (above) resemble a floating bracelet hung along a turquoise-hued coral reef. Boaters are required to tie on to mooring buoys rather than use bottom-disturbing anchors when parked above the Sunshine State's increasingly threatened reefs. Coral reefs are living – and environmentally fragile – ecosystems; some in Florida waters are estimated to be more than two million years old.

Sometimes the keys to capturing a
moment are lots of patience and days of
preparation. In order to catch these three
fledgling ospreys (previous pages) in the act
of being themselves, I had to get permission
from U.S. Coast Guard officials to mount
a remote-control camera on their Severn
River navigation marker in Maryland.
Later I hawked the nest for hours via a
closed-circuit TV camera mounted atop
my film camera. When the young fish
hawks stretched their wings, I finally had
my moment.

  Following the Potomac River below
them, a flock of Canada geese (right)
arrows toward the southeast through the
pale light of a foggy Virginia dawn near
Leesburg. Graceful and elegant in flight,
Canada geese winter in America and
return home to breed in the spring.
Migrating geese can cruise at up to 60 mph.

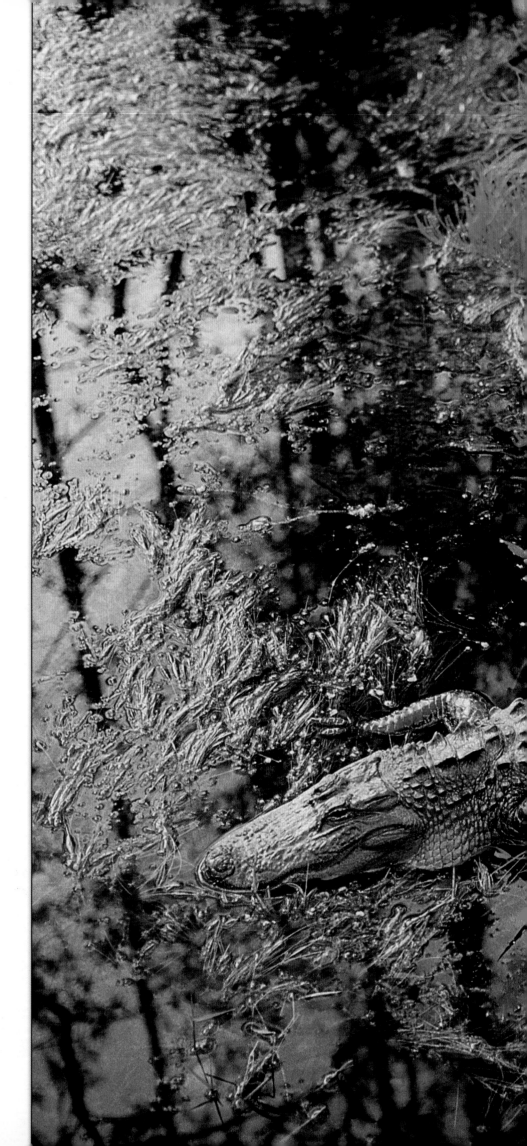

I crept up on this resting alligator in Georgia's Okefenokee Swamp. The big guy didn't seem to mind the sound of my camera snapping open and shut.

But I didn't trust him for a minute. Watching him watch me, I shuddered with the memory of another gator shoot, five years earlier – a photography expedition during which I'd come perilously close to being yanked out of a helicopter by a cousin of this prehistoric-looking monster. It happened on Lake Okeechobee, in the heart of the Florida Everglades, while I was sitting on the floor in the open doorway of a Bell Jet Ranger helicopter.

"Alligator!" I intercommed to the pilot, after spotting a flash of movement. "Let's see how close we can get."

The chopper pilot didn't hesitate. Within seconds we were hovering only two or three yards from the 12-foot-long gator's jaws. I hurriedly switched from a telephoto lens to a wide-angle and then to an even wider one. Our helicopter drifted closer and closer.

That's when he made his move.

Pushing off from a muddy tangle of hydrilla and water lilies, he lunged for my dangling feet. I heard his enormous teeth chomp together, only inches from my toes.

Had the belligerent 1,000-pounder succeeded in clamping onto the helicopter skid, we probably would have ended up with our rotor blade in the drink – en route to becoming the gator's next major meal.

Too close for comfort? Yeah, I'll say.

Along the Atlantic Coast, a wary white-tailed deer scans the terrain around Gordons Pond in Delaware. The U.S. whitetail population has been surging in recent years, in part because of a steep decline in the number of recreational deer hunters. While the ranks of hunters have shrunk, the national whitetail population has soared to more than 20 million, an all-time high. And, as suburbia continues its inexorable sprawl into their habitat, deer sightings in towns and backyard gardens have become increasingly common.

A great egret (right) springs into flight above Augustine Creek in Delaware. The majestic wading birds summer near wetlands, rivers and lakes throughout the country. Like many of their human counterparts, these seasonal wanderers migrate south for the winter. On Florida's Lake Okeechobee, I found this one (following pages) stalking frogs, snakes and fish above a clump of lily pads.

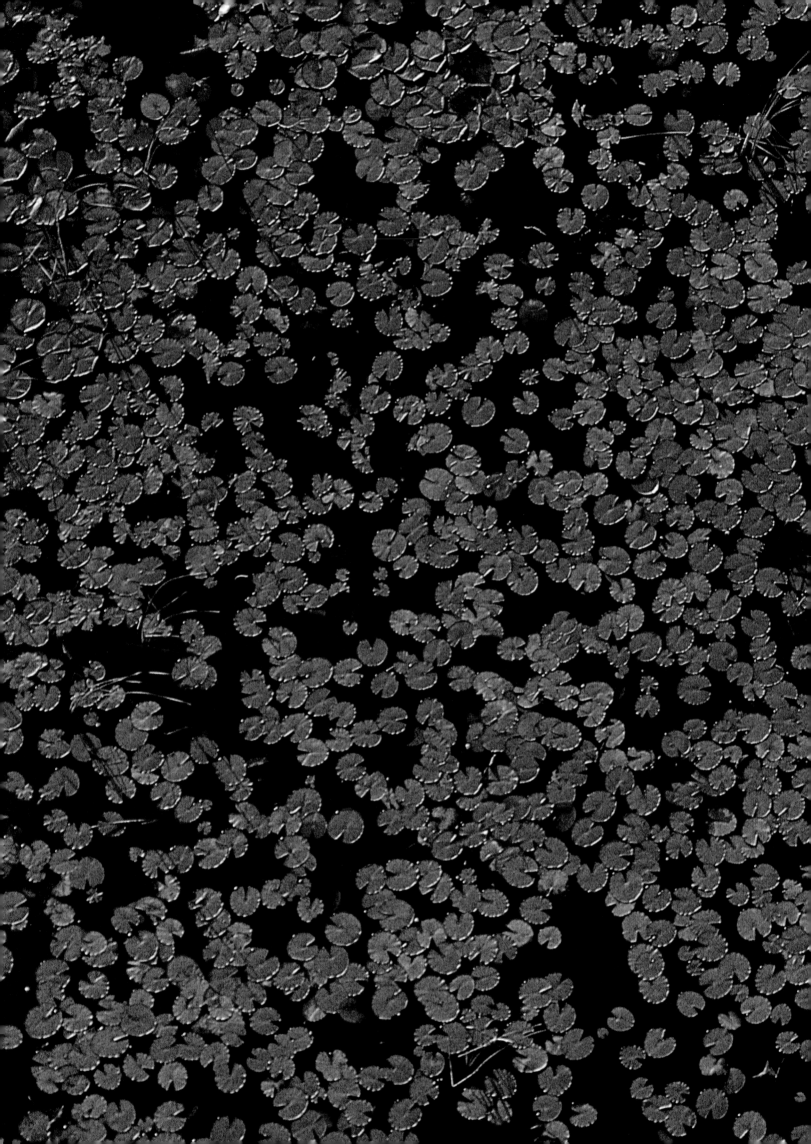

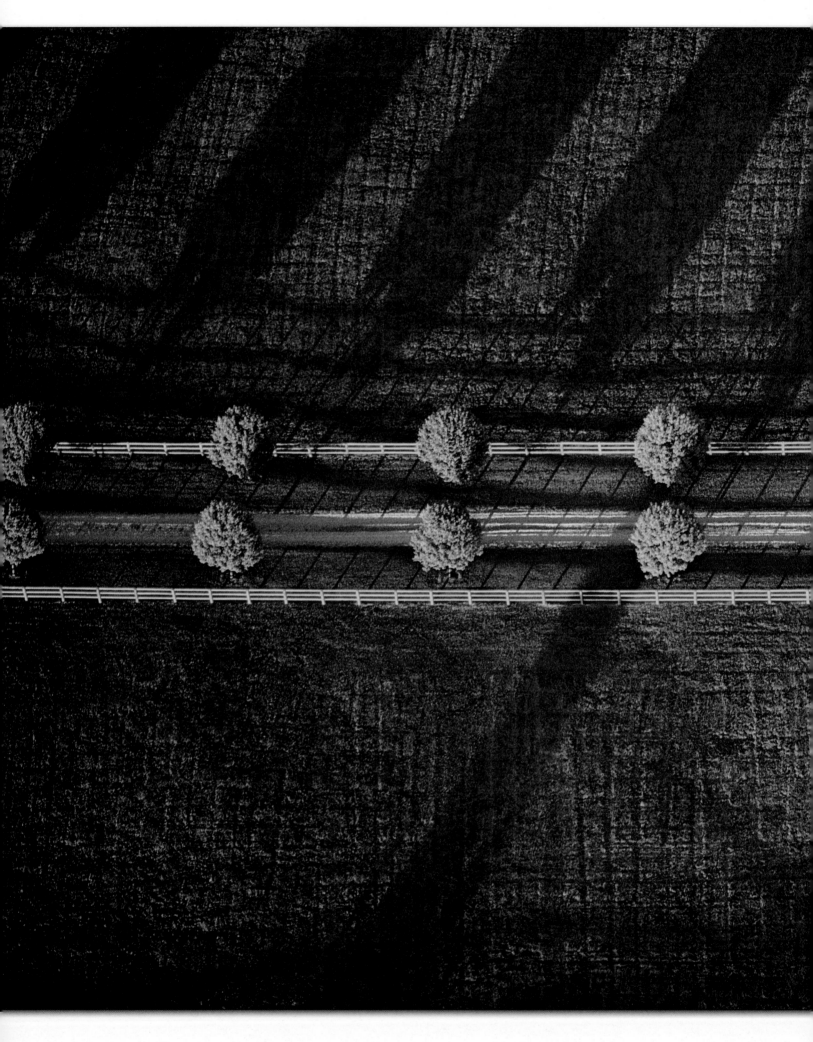

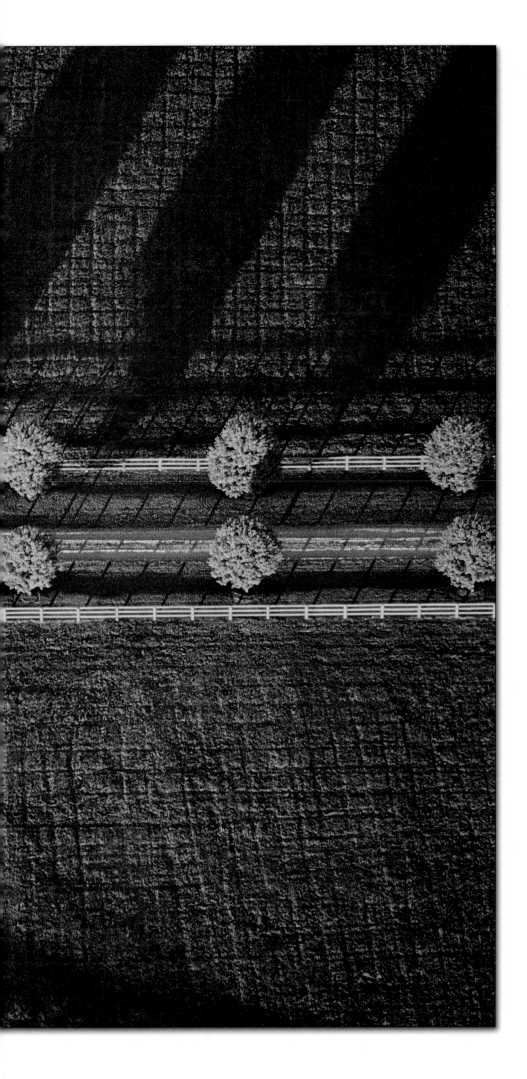

At first glance, you might think nothing much is happening in the photograph. But take a close look at this farm lane in western Maryland (left). From a helicopter I spotted the last rays of sunset lighting up the fence and trees while also casting long shadows onto a hay field. With good light, even the most ordinary subjects like this lane and a Maryland nursery (following pages) seem extraordinary. In photography, as in all of life, there is no substitute for "being there" at the right moment. And sometimes the light is the moment.

Piecing together history with portions of old mills from throughout West Virginia, the Glade Creek Grist Mill (left) was rebuilt in 1976 after a fire destroyed the original structure. Using the fast-running water of Glade Creek for power, the fully operational mill grinds corn, buckwheat and wheat into flour. Early in the 20th century more than 500 mills operated along the creeks of West Virginia.

Taking a scenic tour of Calvert County, Maryland (following pages), a pilot flies a Piper Cub low over farmland highlighted with autumn colors.

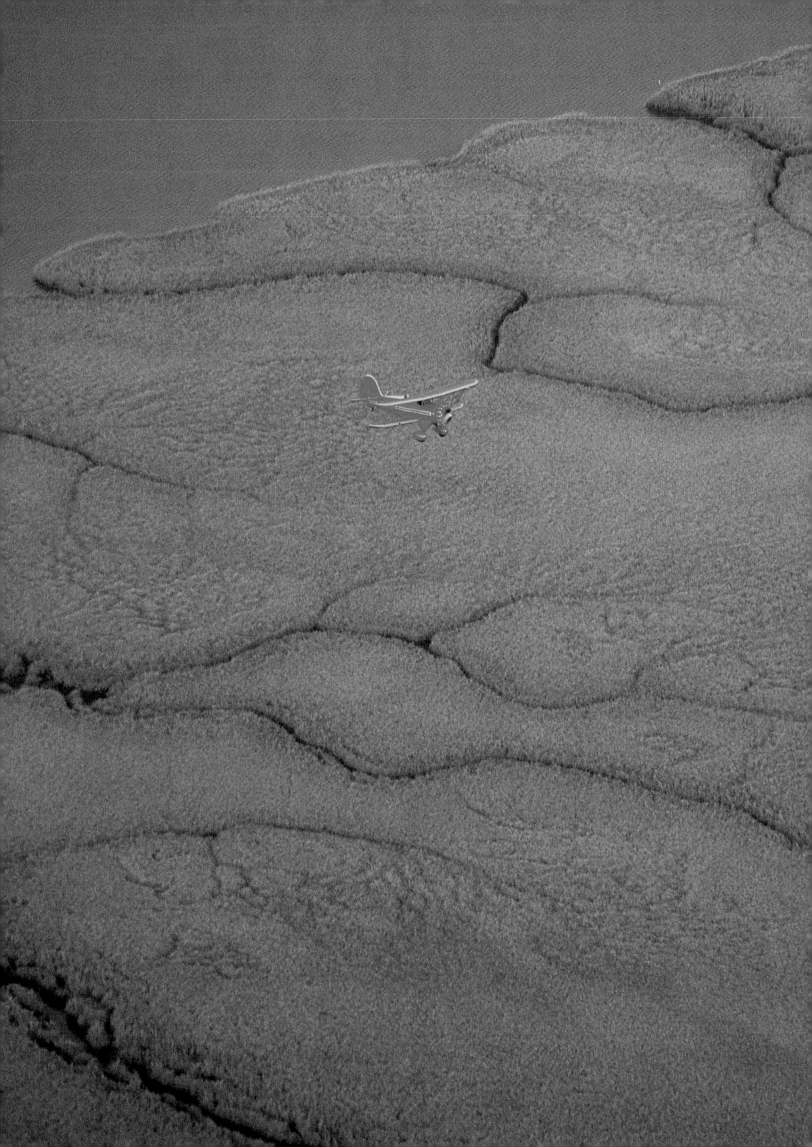

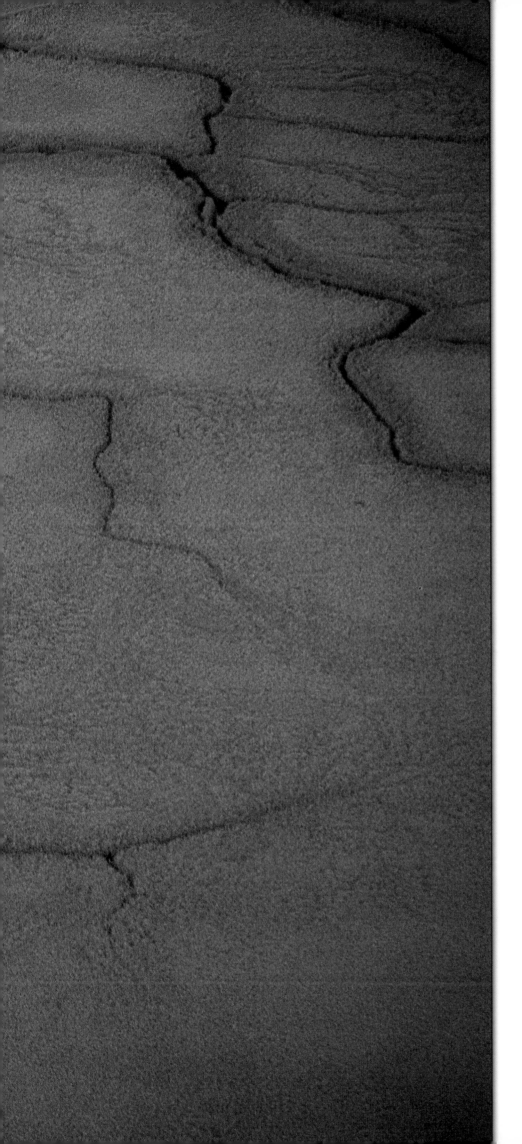

Spend a few weeks flying back and forth across America at 300 or 400 feet, and you'll be amazed at how the land keeps shaping one creative design after the next.

This Georgia salt marsh (left) offers an intriguing example of Mother Earth as illustrator. Strung out along the seacoast near Brunswick, the marshes are cut by wandering creeks. Up close, you'd never notice it – but from the air these meandering streams look exactly like the pale blue veins that transport blood throughout the human body.

While making a coastal flight in his 1934 Waco biplane replica, Georgia attorney and airplane buff James Pleasants (following pages) flew over a wastewater treatment plant operated by Georgia-Pacific.

Following along in a Cessna airplane, I was surprised to see that the paper mill's water treatment ponds and bubbling aerators perfectly resembled microscopic blood cells that would have been carried by the "veins" I'd just observed along the seacoast. Aerial images like these remind me constantly that the earth has a "body" – and that the story of America is first and foremost a story of the land.

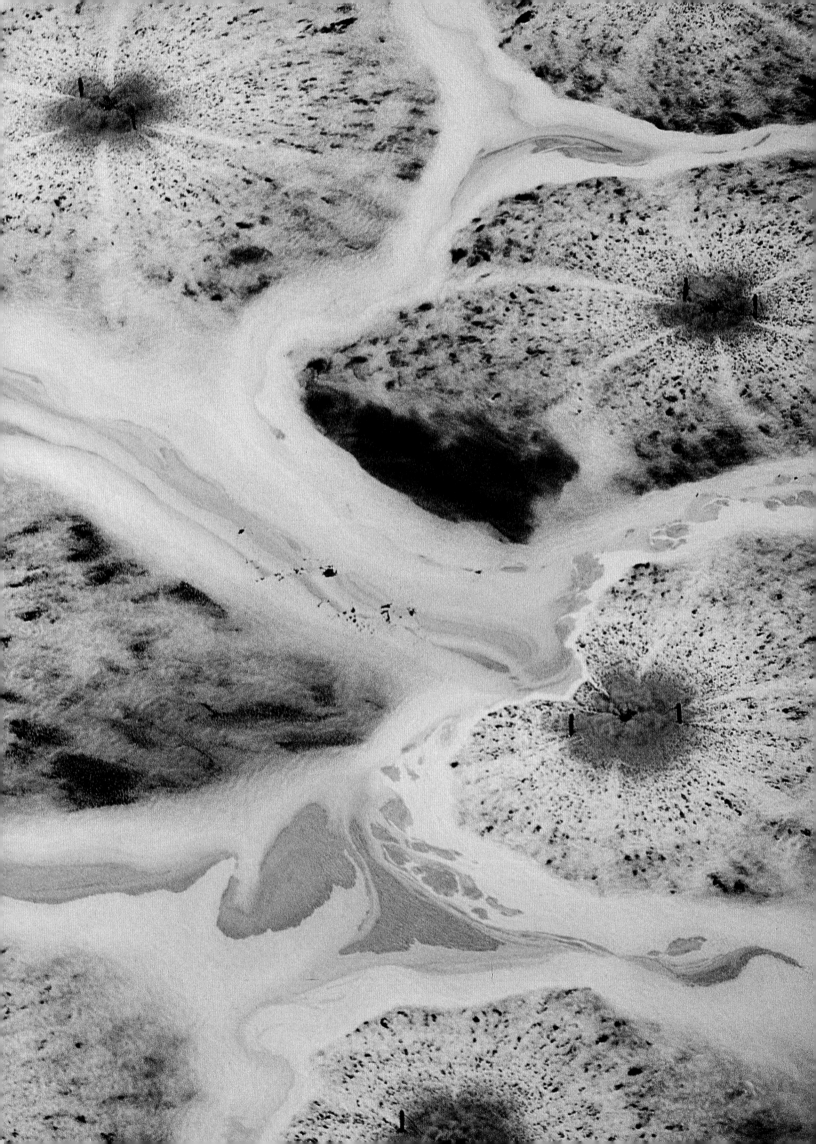

Common throughout the Appalachians, oak trees turn uncommonly beautiful in October, when the leaves of these sturdy hardwoods flare into blazing scarlet and yellow (previous pages).

I spent a week backpacking across remote Isle Royale in Michigan (above and right), a 37-mile-long wilderness haven where motor vehicles are strictly prohibited and packs of timber wolves howl at night. Located in the middle of Lake Superior, the world's largest freshwater lake, the island features 165 miles of backcountry trails. Isle Royale is a North Woods wildlife paradise – yet it attracts fewer visitors each year than Yellowstone draws in a single day. I didn't see another human being the entire week.

Perfect! Intent on capturing the ultimate wild moose or fox photograph, I clambered up jagged rocks and down slippery trails. I found plenty of moose and fox, and shot hundreds of photographs that week. But the images I like most didn't have anything to do with wildlife.

Instead, I found the "native spirit" of Isle Royale in a lake-drenched feather – and in the red, heart-shaped leaves of a vine clinging to the ragged trunk of a paper birch tree.

I was flying along Delaware's Brandywine River Valley one late October afternoon, when all at once I spotted what looked like a giant pumpkin.

"Whoa!" I shouted. "What in the world is that?" Left turn.

Sure enough, someone had carved out a four-and-a-half-acre Jack O' Lantern in the middle of a cornfield. There it was, plain as day to me hovering overhead – but completely invisible to passing drivers. Why would someone go to so much trouble?

Returning by car, I soon caught up with the agrarian artist, Stewart Ramsey Jr. He runs Ramsey's Pumpkin Patch alongside the maze he created to help sell his harvest. "My large cash crop is pumpkins, 12 acres, all retail," he said. "Everybody who went in my maze really liked it but the maze was a failure from an economic standpoint. We didn't have enough awareness. We're going to try again this year and we'll have more going on than paths through a cornfield."

I thought maybe a viewing tower would help, too.

Rimed with an October frost, maple leaves (following pages) glitter beneath the sunrise light on a farm near Georgetown, Delaware.

When nature transforms everyday landscapes into works of art I grab my camera and hit the road. This snowy farm scene near Denton, Maryland (previous pages), looks as if it might have been painted for a Christmas card.

"Growing poinsettias is a pain in the butt," Michael Leubecker, manager of Floral Plant Growers near Middletown, Delaware, told me (left). "They're a long crop and they take a lot of effort." With greenhouses covering 10 acres, the business wholesales about 500,000 of the showy holiday flowers to stores in the mid-Atlantic region. Here, worker Kaorn Caim carries ready-for-market plants through a sea of Freedom Red poinsettias. "When you look at acres of red, white and pink, they are pretty," Leubecker allows. "But they're prettier when they're in someone's home and paid for."

Often described as a "museum without walls," Annapolis, Maryland's state capital, features hundreds of 18th- and 19th–century architectural landmarks. In some areas of the city (population: 35,838), entire blocks have been restored and look almost exactly as they did a century or two ago. First developed in the mid-1700s, Cornhill Street (previous pages) seems frozen in time after a recent snowfall. This block housed city shopkeepers and their clerks during America's Colonial period. Except for the overhead power lines and TV antennas, the setting might have been lifted intact from about 1770.

Like spokes in a giant wheel, the snow-plowed streets of Annapolis (left) radiate toward the Severn River and Chesapeake Bay. Standing tall at the center of State Circle is the oldest capital building in continuous use in the 50 states. The streets of Annapolis resonate with U.S. history: George Washington resigned his Revolutionary War army commission here, and the Founding Fathers gathered for one of the first U.S. Congresses. That happened in 1783 when Annapolis was – for nine months – the capital of the United States.

Towering 275 feet above downtown Des Moines, the Iowa State Capitol (following pages) features a majestic dome gilded with 100 troy ounces of 23-karat gold leaf along with elegant interiors and staircases constructed from 29 different kinds of marble. Total cost of construction, when it was completed in 1886: $2,873,294.59. These days, you'll find the ornate neoclassical dome reflected in the mirrors of a nondescript, box-like office building, a typical example of 1970s-style architecture, directly across the street.

The mirrors seemed pretty slick. But I wonder what those 1886 craftsmen would think of their glitzy new neighbor if they could drop by for a visit.

The big show included stars, flashes, thundering booms and rainbow showers of light (previous pages). And even a "smiley face." Patriotic pyrotechnics galore! I watched twilight fall on Washington, D.C., from the Iwo Jima monument across the Potomac River in Virginia. I could see the Lincoln Memorial, the Washington Monument and the U.S. Capitol and feel the anticipation of almost a million people gathered to watch the annual Independence Day celebration. The U.S. National Park Service didn't disappoint. Rocket after rocket lit the night sky. And, when one gigantic red explosion ever so briefly painted the nation's capital, I knew I had witnessed a special moment.

Over Chicago (right), a pinwheel of blazing fireworks explodes near the landmark Navy Pier. When it comes to pyrotechnics, the "Second City" nickname does not apply. During a recent Memorial Day weekend, Chicagoans could enjoy an impressive show for three nights straight.

Like Piccadilly Circus in London and the Champs Elysées in Paris, Chicago's "Magnificent Mile" radiates excitement and energy as a must-see destination for millions of tourists each year. The action rarely stops along this one-mile stretch of Michigan Avenue, where busy street peddlers hawk souvenirs and trendy boutiques showcase the latest fashions.

The Mile also serves as a kind of an outdoor sculpture museum, with dozens of fiberglass objects – including brightly painted sofas and even this cherry-topped cake (right) – placed artfully along busy sidewalks. I caught these two in the act of taking their own photograph on the Art Deco furniture.

With more than eight million human inhabitants, greater Chicago often seems larger than life. Here you'll find the world's biggest commercial office building (the Merchandise Mart), the biggest aquarium (the Shedd, on Lake Shore Drive), the biggest bakery (Nabisco) – and also the biggest free public zoo (Lincoln Park) on the planet.

All very impressive, to be sure.

But the subjects that fascinate me most in Carl Sandburg's "City of Big Shoulders" are the folks I find by wandering along thoroughfares like Michigan Avenue and in Grant Park where a bride (following pages) kept on walking, unaware that her new husband had stopped for a drink of water.

At first glance, the image suggests triumph, even jubilation: A proud-looking African-American veteran, his automobile festooned with two giant U.S. flags (left), cruises along in a Memorial Day parade in Maryland.

But a closer inspection uncovers a contrast – once you discover that the long rows of grave markers in the background are part of the Annapolis National Cemetery.

This federal burial ground serves as the final resting place for more than 2,500 Union and Confederate soldiers who died fighting in America's most tragic and deadliest conflict. Some lying here fought to keep America together, others battled for separation. The Memorial Day parade was colorful and noisy, a carnival of patriotism. But the distant headstones remained silent.

As a photographer, you never know when you'll suddenly spot your next subject. While listening to the Boston Pops play a Beethoven symphony one evening a few years ago (following pages), I kept an eye on the music lovers who'd gathered on the lawn out front of Boston's renowned Hatch Shell concert stage.

Two things happened. First, I noticed that almost everyone had brought along a blanket to sit on. Second, I speculated that all those blankets, if viewed together, might very well combine to form a giant "human quilt" visible from above.

Next step: I waited a few days for another concert and then rented a helicopter.

I wasn't disappointed. If you drop by the Hatch Shell on the Charles River Esplanade for a major concert – the Earth Day extravaganza in April, maybe, or the annual Fourth of July Boston Pops – you'll find a spot on the colorful human quilt.

It's the biggest street party on the face of the Earth, bar none.

There are endless parades of carnival floats with bourbon-quaffing revelers hurling flashy glass beads from crammed balconies along the streets of New Orleans.

It's *Mardi Gras*, and it's the nearest thing America has to the ancient Roman Circus – a blaring, intoxicating, week-long

festival (left and above) in honor of the rebirth of spring and the beginning of Lent.

Mardi Gras draws more than half a million visitors. On "Fat Tuesday," most seem to be jammed shoulder-to-shoulder on Bourbon Street. It took an hour to move a single block. I spent the day squirming through intoxicated mobs and fighting for enough space to point a camera. It was great!

Perched on the banks of the Ohio River only a few miles north of the Kentucky border, Madison, Indiana, bills itself as "the most beautiful small town in the Midwest."

Driving around the laid-back neighborhoods of drowsy Madison (population 12,004) one summer afternoon, I came upon a man (right) who seemed determined to slow down and savor the picturesque charm of small-town life. For Vern Tandy, there's no better way to spend an afternoon than to bring his own chair from home and settle back to relax in front of Lamson's Feed Store.

The first time I swung past Vern's outpost, around 2 p.m., I told myself: "That's a picture." But the light was bad. When I returned hours later, he still hadn't moved. He told me to go ahead and "shoot all the pictures you want."

So why would a man sit for hours in front of a feed store in southern Indiana? I thought about it for a minute, then decided not to ask. Why spoil a good mystery?

I was scouting out the thriving timber industry near former President Jimmy Carter's Georgia hometown of Plains one afternoon when I flew over a gigantic pile of loblolly pine logs stacked like cordwood around a huge crane. Intrigued, I dropped by the timber-processing company's yard early the next morning to see if I could catch some of the action at ground level.

"We mill lumber for telephone poles and construction companies," the day-shift foreman told me. "It's my job to ride herd on the logs, before the big saws start turning them into two-by-fours."

A moment later, he was leapfrogging toward the middle of his immense log pile. Dwarfed by the soon-to-be-milled trees (right), he looked as if he were playing with a super-sized Lincoln Log set.

Tobacco grower Mack Cashon (following pages) leans into an old door outside his drying shed near Lynchburg, Tennessee. In spite of health risks and government warnings, many farmers still make their living growing and air-curing tobacco leaves in giant sheds like this one.

As twilight falls on western Maryland, a smoker (above) takes a cigarette break outside a general store.

A U.S. Steel worker (right) tends a cascade of molten metal at a steel manufacturing plant in Lorain, Ohio. The temperature outside was well below freezing – but workers at plants with "open pours" like this one don't to have worry about catching a chill. Of much greater concern is the occasional burst of heat from the coke ovens that is powerful enough to set their hair afire.

Did you know that a hungry black bear can scarf down thousands of blueberries in a single day of foraging? It's true – and it's also deeply upsetting for the folks in Washington County, Maine, many of whom make a living by growing and harvesting this delectable fruit every summer.

In this hard-working county, where 90 percent of the nation's blueberries (that's more than 100 million pounds) are processed, local growers take turns picking berries (right) and keeping a wary eye out for the persistent bears.

In Key West, Florida, the southernmost city in the continental United States (population 25,000), tourists and residents alike use the term "sunset" to describe a location, not an event. In Cayo Hueso (Spanish for "Isle of Bone"), "a trip to the sunset" means a late-afternoon visit to Mallory Square to watch the tropical sun drop with surprising rapidity into the turquoise-hued Gulf of Mexico.

But there are plenty of other things to watch here as well – starting with Will Soto. "Will the Juggler" (left) can usually be found walking his high wire as the light fades to indigo and the crowd sends up a traditional round of applause for the sun's daily vanishing act. Bounce the Clown, Madame Ooh La La, Love 22 (who looks like Uncle Sam and hands out $22 bills), The Statue Man (who is usually painted silver and just stands very still), Rick and his Tricky Dogs and Dominique The Cat Man have all graced the "stage" at sunset.

His name: Richard Parker. His game: catching chickens.

When this professional chicken-grabber (previous pages) gets down to business, he doesn't fool around. During 13 years of working for one of America's largest poultry producers – Mountaire Farms, in Millsboro, Delaware – Parker has honed his skills to a razor's edge. By grabbing six or seven pullets at a time, he and five crewmates can empty a 21,000-bird chicken house in less than four hours.

Amish farmers don't drive automobiles or till their fields with tractors. They also shun electricity and modern technology for reasons of religion. But that doesn't mean they aren't good at "kicking the tires" before deciding whether or not to purchase a used one-horsepower vehicle.

I grew up not far from this Amish farm auction in Delaware (right) that brings buyers and sellers together to haggle over plowshares, harnesses, household items and livestock.

After parking their traditional buggies, these farmers got down to some serious dickering over the value of sporty gigs. As a kid, I found my Amish neighbors to be friendly, hard-working folks who were quick to laugh and very resourceful. I still remember being amazed by the ingenuity of one of my Amish teenage buddies – he kept an eight-track tape deck and speakers successfully hidden under the front seat of the family buggy. For him, "old-fashioned" didn't mean behind the times.

I've heard it said that God works in mysterious ways. Few ways seem more unusual than in Sal Verdi's Connecticut back yard (right).

Sal went to bed one night and he had a dream. Being a man of great faith, Sal did exactly what he saw in his dream.

Working mostly alone, he laboriously hand-winched dozens of 300-pound cast-iron bathtubs up the steep hill behind his home. Then he installed a brightly painted concrete Madonna in each of the tubs and adorned his shrines with plastic flowers.

His creation took years to complete. Amazed by his story, I just shook my head. I wondered what his neighbors thought.

Walking with their Jesus, Portuguese-American Catholics (previous pages) celebrate their faith during a festival in Connecticut.

Officiating at a baptism, Pastor Charles Holland immerses one of his New Hope Assembly Church members in the still waters of Trap Pond near Laurel, Delaware (right). "They separate from their sinful life," Holland explained. "When they come to the baptism and say they accept Christ in their lives, that excites me and makes me feel spiritually elevated."

Roper, North Carolina, must be the most churchgoing little town in all of America.

Only 613 people live in this tiny crossroads hamlet on the winding rural highway that connects Raleigh (about 100

miles to the west) with Kitty Hawk and the Outer Banks of the Atlantic seacoast.

In a town this small, you might expect to find only a couple of churches. Not so. I spent a Sunday morning driving the local country roads and came across no fewer than two dozen houses of worship – everything from Holly Neck Church of Christ to Mt. Eprew Missionary Baptist Church to Saints' Delight Church of Christ.

In one of the African-American churches I found a boy (above) who seemed more interested in me and my camera than the service.

Remember that great line in the hit motion picture "Field of Dreams?"

"Is this heaven? No, it's Iowa!"

Chasing the light along Highway 92 – one of Iowa's straight-as-an-arrow country roads – 28 miles west of Winterset, I suddenly found myself in the middle of what looked like a Norman Rockwell landscape. There was an old one-room schoolhouse, a wooden church (left) and a farmer riding an old-fashioned tractor! Was this the town that time forgot?

Not really. As it turns out, the Greenfield County Historical Society is preserving these buildings and the "farmer," Loren Baudler, is actually the groundskeeper.

Ginny Kuhfus proudly told me of the group's efforts to preserve this piece of Iowa history. The Penn Avenue Church is now a favorite wedding spot and the schoolhouse has a new life too. The county kids all have one day of "school" a year in the old building. "It is a new tradition they certainly enjoy," she said.

The annual beauty pageant that selects "Little Miss Millsboro" was about to begin in Delaware and the tiny contestants were doing their best to fend off some major-league stage fright (following pages). While one jittery little miss was being calmed, another crept off into a corner – apparently convinced no one could see her if she kept her face to the wall.

I was out of place here in rural Tunica County, Mississippi, but I don't remember feeling more welcome. People invited me to sit with them and to photograph their children (previous pages).

One lady (right) told me about her decades of "choppin' cotton." I asked what it was like growing up here more than a half-century ago. But she was speechless; she simply couldn't find the words.

I wondered about that. Then I raised my camera and focused on her eyes. They said it all.

I saw this boy's eyes and impassive pose. That was enough for me.

His home (right) was a tiny "shotgun" house in an enclave of former sharecroppers in Tunica County, Mississippi. The ramshackle, unpainted, dusty community seemed to have missed a few decades of progress. Little kids wearing only diapers played outside, oblivious to the Deep South summer heat. Grown-ups sat by a fan or retreated under a porch to seek a respite from the searing sun.

As he looked back at me, I couldn't help but wonder, "What was he seeing?"

Strangers in a strange land? Decked out in Hmong tribal dress, two children (previous pages) help celebrate a recent Fourth of July in Sheboygan, Wisconsin. Nearly 100,000 of these Laotian mountain dwellers were driven out of their homeland and settled in America after Laos fell to the Pathet Lao communist movement at the end of the Vietnam War.

These kids have never seen their native land. In most cases, their parents were uprooted from tribal villages and sent into exile in retaliation for having supported the U.S. military during our war in Indochina.

Like hundreds of thousands of Cambodian and Vietnamese refugees now living from Maine to California, the Hmong provide an exotic thread for the multi-hued tapestry that is America in the new millennium.

When I arrived on the scene in tiny Creswell, North Carolina, I found these Mexican-American migrant farm workers (left) playing with their pet goat.

Ten minutes later, the goat was well on his way to providing the main course for their supper.

But don't let the picture fool you. These youthful cucumber and tomato pickers were living comfortably on a pretty farm. They drove a late-model van and also a second family car (background) in the best American tradition.

In this case, at least, the standard clichés about the hardscrabble life endured by migrant workers in America didn't seem to apply. It seemed a bit strange though, watching their goat go from friendly family pet to entrée. They told me they just love to eat fresh goat.

Whoa, wait a minute – the dog's eating the horse's dinner!

I like it when a photograph tells a story. But what was the story on this Vermont farm (left)? Whose clothes were these? I'll never know, since there was nobody around to ask.

The good news for Outward Bound students on Maine's Hurricane Island (following pages) is that there's not much homework. The hard part is the "classroom" work, which begins at sunrise and goes all day. The school teaches both teamwork and self-reliance with demanding lessons in rock climbing, sailing and backcountry camping.

The American fabric blazes with color wherever you look – and maybe nowhere more than at Dessie Norman's house near Roper, North Carolina (right).

I came upon the Haitian-American artist painting in her front yard late one summer afternoon. Dessie told me she'd had no formal training as an artist, and that she didn't labor over these bright canvases in hopes of selling them. When I gently pressed her to explain why she paints her home and her artwork with such intense colors, she didn't

answer for a moment.

Then, with a smile: "That's what I feel."

William Baxton (above), another self-trained artist, lives not far from Dessie. His North Carolina roots go back many generations and he said he'd never visited the continent of his ancestors or studied their art. Yet he carves powerfully effective four-foot-high ceremonial masks that can only be described as "African." Once they're finished, he proudly exhibits them in the local barbershop and auto garage.

This remarkable wood-sculptor couldn't tell me how he learned to make his masks. "I just do them," he said.

I made one of my fastest U-turns ever after
spotting this camouflaged roller-skating
rifleman (right) patrolling an abandoned
outpost at sunset in Fort Davis, Alabama.
  He was just a boy. What was he doing
with a gun? The gun was a toy, everything
else was real enough. Turns out he was just
playing army, all by himself.

Ray Thompson (left) lives as high in the sky as he possibly can. He built his cabin at the very top of an Appalachian peak near Princeton, West Virginia, where he and his Dalmatian share an incredible view. Some people who have seen this photograph think Ray shares something else – an uncanny resemblance to movie star Sean Connery.

Don't tell 80-year-old Walter DeVore (above) that he should be in retirement. After 65 years of plowing, planting and harvesting his farmstead near Harrison, Arkansas, the feisty agrarian is going stronger than ever.

So what's the secret behind his longevity? "Lots of hard work!"

In economically depressed Bayou La Batre, Alabama – 20 miles south of Mobile, on the Gulf of Mexico – many of the shrimp boats have been idled by falling prices, weakening the economy of the entire area.

Watching these determined kids work hand lines from a rickety pier (previous pages), I wondered if they were crabbing for recreation or for a meal.

When you're living on the edge, the size of your dinner depends – literally – on the size of your catch.

The "cat fishermen" of Florida's 700-square-mile Lake Okeechobee (right) spend many months each year living in lean-tos beside the water. During daylight hours, they bait dozens of lines and drop them into the second-largest body of fresh water in the United States.

At night, they settle back and wait for the lake's catfish to take the bait. The whiskered fish looks a bit strange but its flavorful meat is a favorite seafood choice in restaurants all across the country. But the life of a catfishing family isn't easy – especially when the tropical rains of the Everglades turn their world into a sea of boiling mud.

I caught up with this family at twilight. While supper fried on a camp stove (catfish, of course), the family watched an old black-and-white TV that had been clipped to a car battery. The canvas and plastic lean-to looked comfortable enough…until I heard and felt a swarm of hungry "skeeters" that turned up at twilight.

When I asked if they used "repellent" to drive off the ferocious mosquitoes, a couple of the veteran fishermen laughed out loud.

196

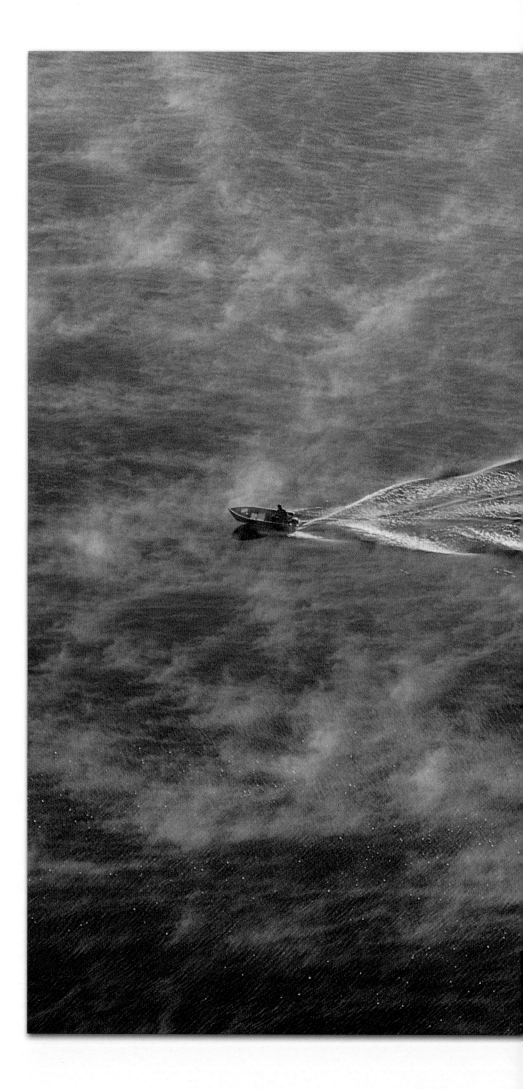

Welcome to the heart of Dixie, just 15 miles from the snarl of morning rush hour traffic in and around metropolitan Atlanta. They take sport fishing very seriously in Georgia, as evidenced by this bass fisherman waking a sleepy Stone Lake while commuting to his favorite fishing hole (right).

Far to the north in Rhode Island, Narragansett Bay provides a significant amount of the yearly catch for the state's $75-million-a-year hard clam and fishing industry.

Like most inland bays, the Narragansett has been increasingly threatened by industrial pollution in recent years, but you'd never know from this peaceful image (previous pages) of sunlit seawater lapping gently against fishing boats.

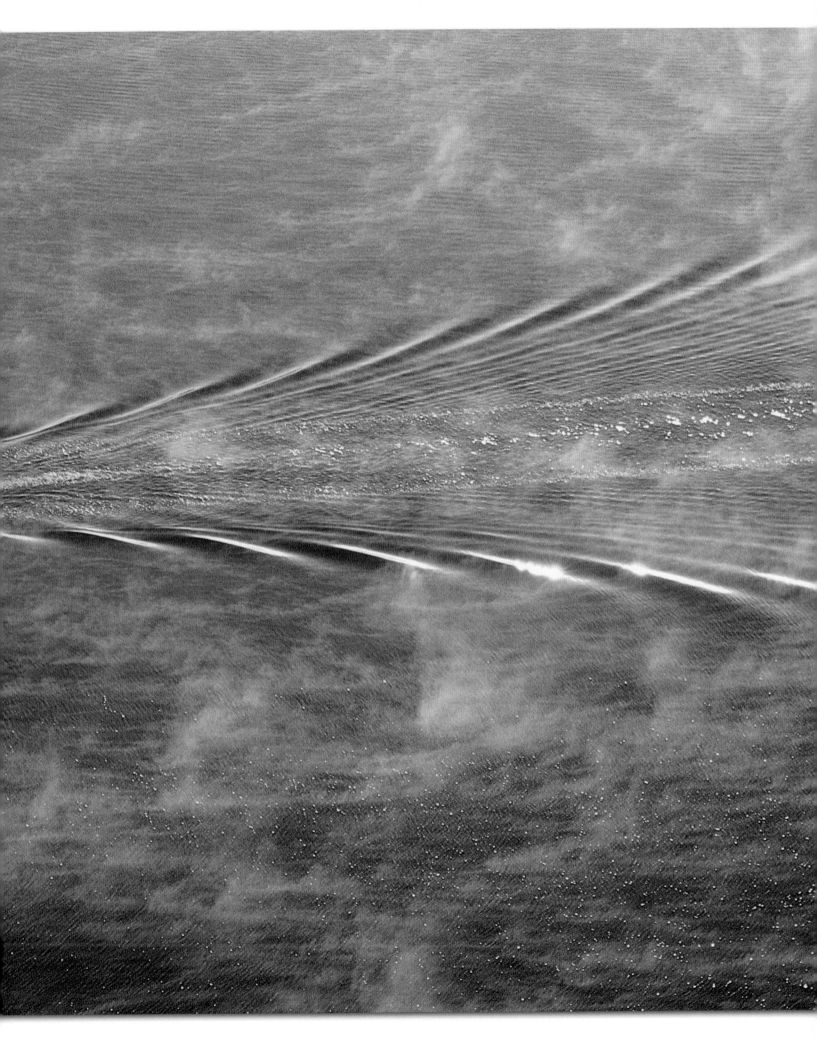

It happened in 1846, along the storm-battered
Outer Banks on the coast of North Carolina.

The legend in a nutshell: A sailing vessel
en route to the Carolinas from Bermuda
ran head-on into a howling hurricane.
After battling the tempest for many hours,
the terrified mariners found themselves
drifting helplessly toward the raging surf
near Cape Hatteras, better known to sailors
as the "Graveyard of the Atlantic."

Then a miracle took place.

At the last moment, just before they capsized,
an immense wave rose out of the storm and
flung their ship a hundred yards inland,
where it landed safely atop a shallow sand
bar. They were saved! And when dawn
broke the next day, they discovered that
the powerful winds and waves had cut a
wide passageway from the Atlantic Ocean
into Pamlico Sound on the western side of
the narrow barrier island.

And the name of their ship? It was
the "Oregon."

These days, that same passageway is
known as Oregon Inlet – and dozens of
sport and commercial fishing boats motor
through the inlet at dawn each day (right)
en route to the Atlantic Ocean.

I wonder how many of today's fishermen
know about the miracle that saved the sailors.

What a clever idea. By renting a slot in this
boatel – "a hotel for boats" – on Maryland's
South River (following pages), owners forever
escape the ordeal of scraping barnacles
and painting hulls. Boatels also solve the
perennially expensive problem of dock
space since the powerboats are stored high
and dry and then plucked out and lowered
on demand for a cruise.

Smart!

And lucky too, for me. Through sheer
coincidence, these red-striped boats perfectly
framed the workman at the center of the
picture.

It's amazing – the way man and nature
combine so often to paint abstract images.

When I flew over these Chesapeake Bay rental rowboats at sunrise in Sandy Point State Park, Maryland (previous pages), I was struck by the inky-black water and the contrasts of the sun-rimmed rental boats tied along the docks.

My work had been done for me; all I had to do was snap the shutter. The diagonals, the parallels and the shapes of the boats instantly reminded me of leaves on a bamboo branch.

What's in a name?

It's Christmas on Carroll's Creek and that's Jubilee leading the way (right).

They call it the "Christmas Lights Parade" and it takes place each December in Annapolis, Maryland.

More than 60 sailboats and powerboats, each decked out with hundreds of blazing Yuletide lights, come floating down the Severn River, then swing past City Dock and up Carroll's Creek. While the crowd (more than 30,000, most years) sings impromptu choruses of Christmas carols, the brilliantly trimmed watercraft compete for bragging rights and prizes handed out by the Eastport Yacht Club.

One by one they pass. Name by name. Jubilee, Dreamchaser and the one I could best relate to on this bitterly cold winter night, Wind Chill.

More than 40 world-class Hobie 16 catamaran racers (following pages) skim across the turquoise surface of Delaware's Rehoboth Bay during the North American Continental Championships.

Exhilarating? You better believe it. Hobies can reach 2.5 times the wind speed and in any decent breeze the windward hull is flying out of the water.

Racing a Hobie requires two experienced sailors. While the "skipper" rides the trampoline and steers, the "crew" hangs far out over the water, hooked onto the end of a trapeze wire.

I was wandering around a Louisiana shipyard one bright spring afternoon when I caught a glimpse of what looked like the World's Largest Wrench (left). I also noticed how the lines of the nearly completed ship flowed toward the porthole where the wrench man was doing his thing.

Once again, the landscape had "composed" the image for

me. All I had to do was wait for the moment when he and the wrench were framed by the ship.

In Maryland, Baltimore Marine Industries services and repairs even larger ships (above). Early one morning, I found workers polishing and fine-tuning a huge bronze propeller. And, although I didn't see one, I bet they have even larger wrenches.

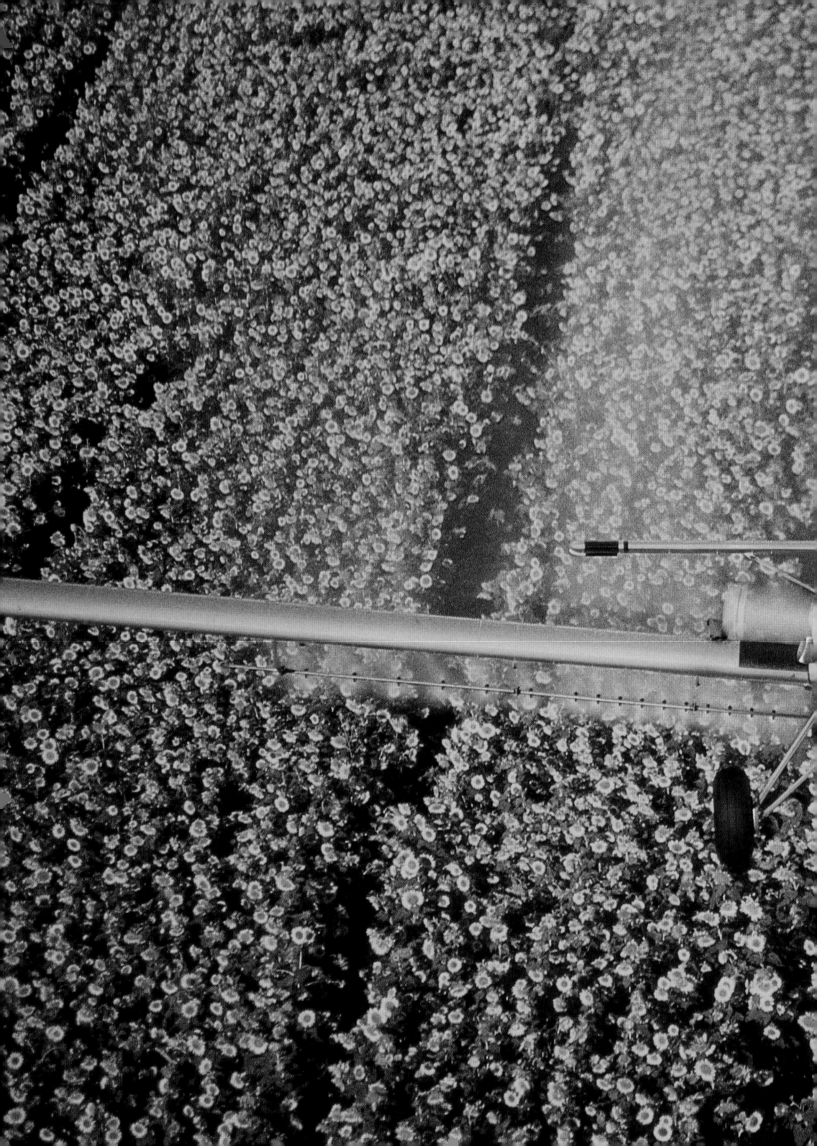

Engine roaring and propeller spinning, the 600–horsepower Ayres S2R Thrush crop–duster was flying straight for me at a speed of better than 130 mph (previous pages). I was stuck 40 feet up in the air in the electric company's "bucket" truck and there was nowhere to go.

Yikes!

Gritting my teeth, I started shooting. But it wasn't easy. Only two years before, while taking photographs from a similar bucket truck in Charleston, South Carolina, I'd taken the kind of horrendous fall you never forget.

Knocked off balance in a freak accident, the truck had turned over on its side – and I rode the bucket down through a 45-foot freefall that ended in a hard crash on the sidewalk.

That accident left me with a broken back . . . and months of painful rehabilitation.

Somehow, I managed to get this photograph.

Then the airplane flew straight over my head. It seemed like just inches. The "wake turbulence" grabbed my bucket and shook it hard enough to rattle my bones.

Two hours later pilot Allen Chorman laughed out loud when I told him about the experience.

"What the heck were you worried about?" barked the jovial Chorman. "Hey, I cleared you by a good three feet!"

Looking ghostly as a desert mirage, a commercial passenger jet lifts off Runway 28 at Baltimore-Washington International Airport just before sunrise (right). The two-mile stretch of tarmac was still warm from baking in the previous day's midsummer sun and heat waves reflected the landing lights.

What you're seeing is a Delaware Air National Guard C-130 Hercules about to touch down on Runway 1 at New Castle Airport. The versatile turboprop can carry 42,000 pounds of cargo or 92 combat troops.

What you're not seeing is the special housing unit built to hold my camera atop the tail of the aircraft and the mountain of paperwork required to get it there. This short flight needed a series of permissions moving through the military chain of command in Delaware to the Adjutant General and up through the Pentagon.

It all came together for a couple of seconds on final approach. While the big plane streaked toward the runway at better than 100 mph (right), I sat in the cockpit and shot photographs from the tail by remote control. What I wanted was the image you're looking at – a phantasmagoric blur of streaking runway lights captured by a super wide-angle lens and a very slow shutter speed. But would my strategy work?

I waited in suspense while the film was developed.

Then a technician called from the photo lab. "Hey, Kevin – one of these shots looks really cool!"

Good thing. I only had one shot at it.

Lined up nose to nose (following pages), a dozen monster-sized C-5 Galaxy cargo planes stand poised for flight at Dover Air Force Base in Delaware.

Everything about these airborne work-horses seems larger than life – starting with the size of the cargo they can haul. Easily able to transport six Greyhound buses at a time, the Lockheed-manufactured planes were designed to schlep 291,000 pounds of military supplies at more than 500 mph and still land safely on less than a mile of runway.

As for fuel, don't even ask. It takes 332,500 pounds – more than six railroad tank cars – to fill up, so you better bring all your credit cards. And the purchase price? Only $167 million, right off the showroom floor.

I wondered if the Wright brothers could have envisioned these giants. Their entire first flight could have taken place inside a C-5.

Three dozen of the nation's 126 C-5s are stationed at Dover. First operational in 1970, they are the backbone of the U.S. military's global transportation system.

The 4,000 midshipmen who attend the U.S. Naval Academy in Annapolis, Maryland (previous pages), have a special name for the odd behavior you see here.

They call it "grazing."

But not to worry. Grazing is actually pretty common at the Academy. Each May when the midshipmen shoulder their rifles and unsheath their swords in order to practice for graduation, they're warned not to "lock" their knees rigidly while standing at attention.

Lock your knees, and you choke off the circulation of blood back to your brain.

Then you faint. And you graze.

A slippery rite of passage at the Naval Academy marks the end of freshman year for fourth-class midshipmen, called plebes. Muscles strain as a human pyramid (right) grows around Herndon Monument, greased with 200 pounds of lard and crowned with a "dixie cup" hat worn by plebes. Tradition has it that whoever scales the obelisk and places an upperclassman's hat on top is destined to become the class's first admiral.

The "Corps of Cadets" drills on the Quad at The Citadel (following pages). Although the 1,900 cadets who attend this venerable military college (founded in 1842) in Charleston, South Carolina, don't belong to the U.S. military, they're all required to take ROTC. Many do go on after graduation to accept commissions as officers in the U.S. Army.

Steeped in tradition, The Citadel often stages colorful parades and exercises on the red and white squares of the college's parade deck or "Quad."

In 1861, a group of cadets from The Citadel earned a permanent place in history by firing the first shots of the Civil War at a federal cargo ship delivering supplies to Fort Sumter.

Except for the Bible, **<u>The Adventures of Huckleberry Finn</u>** is probably the most popular book in the entire history of the American Republic.

Who hasn't flipped open Mark Twain's classic 1885 novel – and then thrilled to the escapades of the unforgettable Huckleberry Finn? In Hannibal, Missouri, birthplace of Mark Twain (a.k.a. Samuel Langhorne Clemens), they honor the memory of his most famous creation with a yearly festival known as "Huck Finn Days." One winner of the Huck Look-Alike Contest (right) carried a fishing pole in one hand and a bullfrog in the other – while puffing contentedly on his trademark corncob pipe.

I wonder what Mark Twain would have written to describe the rodeo band playing at the Kansas State Fair in Hutchinson (above). Maybe something like, "playing 'til the cows come home" or possibly "playing to a captive audience." Either way, these Herefords had a front-row seat for the performance but had to face the music again later as they were the main event in the calf-roping competition.

Okay, everybody: Will the real little girl please raise her hand?

(Hint: She's the one with the Tootsie Pop – and the colorful tongue.)

I was on Main Street in downtown Mitchell, South Dakota (home of the "World's Only Corn Palace"), one summer afternoon, when I happened upon a woman who makes lawn statues out of cement. Lots and lots of lawn statues.

After pouring the wet stuff into special molds and waiting several days for it to dry, she paints her elves and gnomes and trolls in bright colors.

When the sculptor's two-year-old daughter wandered into the scene – while slurping a grape-flavored Tootsie Pop – I reached for my camera. Her tongue was painted the same purple hue as the statues and for a moment she blended right in (right).

The headlines may change each day, but not the ritual of delivering the morning paper at the crack of dawn.

Here in Mitchell, South Dakota, the paper is the Daily Republic (circulation: 12,000). Watching the early light breaking all around Nathaniel Torbertson (left) as he delivered a satchel full of papers from door to door, I caught a glimpse of the newspaper logo. It was, of course, a sunrise.

Neatly framed by her daddy's blue pickup, two-year-old Devon Ward (previous pages) offers the camera her Mona Lisa smile on a dirt road outside Zinc, Arkansas, in the heart of the Ozarks.

Question: Who shotgunned this gentleman's truck?

I was rattling along a bumpy road in the rough-and-tumble Arkansas Ozarks when I spotted a man pushing an old tractor tire across a field of buttercups (left). Looking more closely, I noticed that the truck had been pockmarked with buckshot.

U-turn!

As I approached the farmer, I was remembering how, a century earlier, these same rugged Arkansas mountains had provided hide-outs for some of America's most notorious outlaws – including Jesse James, Bonnie and Clyde, and even Pretty Boy Floyd.

But the tire-pusher turned out to be a perfectly sensible and friendly farmer named Gary Richardson. He spent a few hours showing me around his farm near Harrison and telling me about the spectacular scenery to be found throughout his beloved Ozarks.

So far, so good. But when I asked him who had riddled his truck with gunfire, he only shrugged.

Apparently, catching a little buckshot now and then was a routine event in his part of the world.

In tiny Jasper, Arkansas, several of the locals suggested that I visit a real "hillbilly," Nick Ray, and his "neat old farm" outside town.

I hurried out there and found Nick flinging cracked corn to his chickens while his wife Janet hovered in the doorway of their farmhouse (left).

The Rays lacked many modern comforts, including indoor plumbing, and their home was insulated with pages from a 1937 Saturday Evening Post glued to the wall. But they couldn't have been more gracious and generous hosts. I spent two days photographing their kids, their chickens, their goats and even their Vietnamese pot-bellied pigs.

Round 'em up – and give 'em a long drink of water (previous pages)!

After 200 straight days without rain, these undersized cows looked about as parched as the West Texas landscape on which they had been grazing.

As soon as I stepped onto this dusty feedlot at Dumas – about 60 miles north of Amarillo in the desert-like Texas Panhandle – I felt the drought too. It was hard to imagine how cowboys worked here day after day in the heat and choking dust.

When Bill White's ancestors first began developing his 20,000-acre cattle ranch on the Gulf of Mexico near Galveston (left), the year was 1811 and James Madison was president. Nearly two centuries later, White carries on the tradition, raising cattle and growing wheat, oats and rye, storing the grain in immense, multi-story grain elevators.

To me, the Spirit of America felt alive and
well on a cattle ranch in northern California.

While 12-year-old John Periano (right)
gazed thoughtfully into my lens, his hard-
working parents were busy branding cattle
behind me. The Periano cattle business in
the Sierra Nevada foothills stretches back
through five generations – all the way back
to the American Civil War.

I could see the strength, determination
and dedication of John's ancestors right
there on his young face.

In the American West, they have more sky
than anything else. They have more of
something else too. Windmills. And no
one has more than J.B. Buchanan (following
pages). Still spry at age 90, he maintains
the 13 windmills in his collection near
Stinnett, Texas. Long before electricity hit
the West, windmills converted prairie
winds into the energy needed to pump
water for homesteaders and livestock. J.B.
told me as a boy he remembered how a
running windmill sounded like music and
gave him a feeling of comfort and security.
As the breeze picked up, I looked up at J. B.
and thought he must be feeling very secure.

A symphony was playing in his back yard.

"Good-bye, God, I'm going to Bodie," lamented a young girl in her diary when she learned her family was moving to the wildest of the California gold-rush towns. One preacher summed up the notorious town as a "sea of sin, lashed by the tempest of lust and passion." Murders allegedly occurred about once a day until June 1881, when the Bodie Free Press reported that "Bodie is becoming a quiet summer resort – no one killed here last week."

It was definitely quiet the morning I visited Bodie (right). A snowstorm made the last two miles of the narrow High Sierra mountain road (8,200 feet above sea level) impassable by car, so I had to hike in. Standing knee-deep in the cold and snow of a ghost town, the Old West seemed a very long time ago.

I left snow-choked Bodie that morning and threaded my way south through the jagged Sierra Mountains reaching Death Valley (following pages) just in time for sunset. It was 100 degrees hotter on this scorched lunar–like landscape and 282 feet below sea level. The names on my map told me all I wanted to know about the agonies endured by many of California's pioneers – Coffin Canyon, Funeral Peak and Suicide Pass.

Make a mistake on this sand-whipped and waterless terrain and you died. Period. No mercy and no second chance. But they went anyway, didn't they?

Looming high atop a 367-foot sandstone monolith, New Mexico's Acoma Pueblo is regarded by most historians as the "oldest inhabited village" in the United States. Today the Pueblo (left) is home to a thriving Native American settlement and one of the country's best-known cultural and historical museums.

Centuries before the first Europeans arrived in the New World, the Acomas and other pueblo-dwellers were living in these mud-brick houses. This tribe gained fame throughout the Southwest for its exquisite, thin-walled pottery.

What happened to the mysterious cliff-dwellers of Mesa Verde? For more than 700 years (600-1300 A.D.), a now-vanished community of Native Americans inhabited the cliff-sides at "Green Table," near contemporary Cortez, Colorado. Then, within the space of two generations in the late 1200s, they vanished without a trace. Today, 24 different Native American tribes in the Southwest claim to have ancestral links back to Mesa Verde (above).

With a million-dollar view but few of life's amenities, Leo Yellowhair (left) lives on the rim of Arizona's rugged Coal Mine Canyon. A Navajo squatting on Hopi land, Leo spends his days tending 18 sheep. He told me he sells their wool to get the $25 he needs to have water delivered twice a month. Leo didn't use many words to tell me about his life in the desert. He didn't have to, as everything already was reduced to simple elements.

In nearby Window Rock, Navajo Steven Benally Jr., (above) is studying to be a healer (the non-Native American term is "medicine man") who will commune with the "spirit world" in order to overcome illness by bringing the patient back into harmony (*hozho*) with nature.

Navajo healers use sand paintings that depict creation stories, along with feathers, herbs and other medications while practicing their craft. His scars are from a traditional sundance ceremony representing life and rebirth.

A Navajo mother (below) pauses for a quiet moment from her job as a shepherd in the Arizona desert. Nearby, in Window Rock (right), Navajo kids prefer to spend the afternoon bouncing on a trampoline.

The Navajo Nation has bounced back as well. Numbering only 8,000 in the 1860s, the Navajo population now totals more than 210,000 with 60 percent age 24 or younger.

Navajo elder Mary Watchman (below) holds on to her young granddaughter Tanisha Begay in their Fort Defiance, Arizona home. Looking into their eyes that matched so closely, I felt I could see their ancestors as well.

In rural Montana (right), at a mountain man festival celebrating the culture and traditions of the Old West, I found another Native American concentrating on braiding her grandson's hair. Looking into his eyes, as he winced in pain from her firm grip, I could see one tradition he might prefer to forget.

Drive the endless roads of the Navajo Nation in New Mexico, and you'll cruise past dozens of outdoor jewelry stores like this one (left). These boys spend their days hawking "dreamcatchers," which are cleverly designed to allow friendly, uncomplicated dreams to slip easily through the round opening in the device – while tangled, twisted nightmares get hung up in the webbing and then perish with the first light of day.

The roadside stands also feature silver and turquoise amulets, pendants, bracelets and ceremonial canes crafted by Navajo artisans.

About 20 miles from Mexican Hat, Utah, I found a stark scene that perfectly captured the beauty – and the unforgiving harshness – of America's Old West.

Monument Valley, which stretches from Utah well into neighboring Arizona, provides an astonishing landscape dominated by the Twin Mittens, freestanding, sandstone rock formations that soar to a height of more than 1,000 feet above the desert floor. It's no accident that such classic John Wayne westerns as "Stagecoach" (1939) were filmed with these giant monoliths in the background.

Exploring the desolate valley, I spotted a horse's sun-bleached skeleton (right) resting on the dusty desert floor. The sun was just breaking when I approached the remains, and rays briefly illuminated the ribs of the long-dead steed.

I caught the light and then sat quietly for a few minutes thinking about the courage of the pioneers who first dared to cross this formidable desert and Monument Valley. This is exactly what they saw.

Spooky? You bet. And these weird-looking rock formations in southern Utah's Bryce Canyon National Park (following pages) have been wonderfully named – they're called "hoodoos."

Shaped by millions of years of wind and rain erosion, the hoodoos also carry technical, geological monikers, such as "spires," "fins," "pinnacles" and "mazes." I made this photograph just before twilight, when the last fiery rays of the declining sun were bathing the sandstone and limestone towers in pale, unearthly magenta.

Welcome to the Twilight Zone, for real.

Imagine their campfire, 150 years ago. The moon hangs like a tiny beacon above a distant sandstone butte. A light breeze at dawn riffles through the branches of the overhanging cottonwood tree.

This is what American pioneers must have seen (left) – the awesome emptiness of the land they hoped to settle. Crossing Utah's Monument Valley, did they sit beside their fires and talk about the fearsome challenges that lay ahead? Did they appreciate the beauty of this desert or could they only feel the harshness and see the obstacles?

One thing is certain: At first light, they loaded their wagons and moved on. They had a new world to build, and they could not afford to linger here.

The Colorado River (following pages) knifes its way through granite bedrock in Canyonlands National Park, Utah. It took a billion years of river erosion to create many of the cliffs and canyons that form the heart of this 338,000-acre federal preserve.

Question: How long is a billion years?

Answer: Consider this interesting fact. The Colorado had already been gnawing away at the bedrock for *700 million years* when the dinosaurs made their first appearance at the start of the Triassic Era.

In geological time, the dinosaurs showed up about half an hour ago.

And humans? Don't even ask.

The mighty Colorado, the major river of the American Southwest, drains 242,000 square miles of land and funnels most of it through the narrow, mile-deep Grand Canyon in Arizona. During its plunge through the canyon, the river takes a 2,200-foot nosedive, triggering a series of Level 3 and Level 4 rapids guaranteed to make most first-time rafters scream their lungs out (left).

Riding the boiling whitewater was lots of fun but the nights were even more memorable. Falling asleep on the canyon floor, I gazed at rock walls that had taken entire geologic epochs to form. . . and then found myself hypnotized by dozens of satellites crossing the night sky high above. The dry, clean desert air was so clear that stars, constellations, satellites and even galaxies were visible to the naked eye.

During that week on the Colorado, I went to sleep every night at the bottom of a billion years, looking into forever.

More than 275 miles long and 19 miles wide in places, the Grand Canyon is frequently described as "the most popular scenic attraction" on Earth. It also ranks number one among the Seven Natural Wonders of the World and holds a commanding lead over the runner-up, Mount Everest.

I made this photograph (previous pages) from South Rim, just as the deep purple of twilight settled over the vast stone labyrinth that houses the billion-year-old canyon and river bed some 5,000 feet below.

I would guess all five million visitors to the canyon are touched by the experience. Standing at the edge of Mother Nature's most impressive work, it is easy to understand why.

Sometimes you have to work pretty hard to get the photograph you want (previous pages).

First, I rented a pair of snowshoes in Jackson Hole, Wyoming. Then, before dawn, I hiked across the tundra until I found Moulton Barn. Built in the late 1800s by a Mormon homesteader, the barn is now part of Grand Teton National Park.

After a snowshoe-struggle of about 45 minutes, I was drenched in perspiration. And I was early. (The temperature: one degree Fahrenheit.) Shivering with cold, I waited for nearly half an hour, until at last. . . the dawn broke and it was all worthwhile.

A True Sense of Scale: How'd you like to live in a place where the temperature sometimes dips to minus 46F in January, and you get pelted with more than 140 inches of snow each winter?

Welcome to the Grand Teton Mountain Range in Wyoming. If you enjoy bust-a-gut mountain-climbing, the 13,770-foot Grand Teton summit may be for you. Or rattle your jawbone on a plunging whitewater-ride through the Snake River Canyon, also a favorite activity among visitors to Grand Teton National Park.

A third possibility: Just sit quietly and meditate on this majestic landscape. Can you find the horseback rider and the pack horse on the steep mountain slope? (left) *Tiny*, aren't they?

It happens late every autumn, when the lower slopes of Wyoming's Grand Tetons begin to blaze with leaves of burnt orange and bright vermilion (following pages).

That's the vivid backdrop for an estimated 7,500 of these deer "cousins" that winter in the nearly 25,000-acre National Elk Refuge near Jackson Hole. Snowfall in the high country prompts the elk to move from their summer ranges to lower elevations.

Mono Lake, California, (previous pages) gets my vote as the most surreal landscape in America. Here's why:

The ancient lake – a saline oasis on the edge of Great Basin desert a mile above sea level in California's Eastern Sierra – percolates with minerals leached from ancient volcanoes.

These minerals, especially calcium, bubbled up from the floor of the lake for hundreds of years and mixed with carbonates in the water forming underwater limestone towers or "tufas."

When the City of Los Angeles began diverting the freshwater streams that feed the lake a few decades ago, the water level declined rapidly, exposing a bizarre, alien landscape.

What a great movie set this would make for a sci-fi thriller. Certainly Hollywood filmed dozens of outer-space epics here. Mono Lake looks exactly like the place Martians, Ewoks or Jabba the Hut would call home.

Not so, it turns out.

Only a couple have been filmed here, none with space invaders. But Clint Eastwood did wander across this forbidden landscape in "High Plains Drifter."

Water, water everywhere . . . and this nervy kayaker (right) wouldn't have it any other way.

The waterfall he's enjoying can be found on a roaring tributary of the Snake River, not far from Jackson Hole, Wyoming. Does the scene look familiar? Robert Redford shot part of his 1992 fly-fishing epic, "A River Runs Through It," along this trout-filled waterway.

This one I couldn't believe.

I noticed a blooming yellow canola field on my way to Driggs, Idaho. But it was mid-afternoon with harsh light, a clear blue sky and nothing was happening.

I stopped in Driggs and ordered lunch. Waiting for my meal, I watched the sky suddenly begin to darken (right). Summer thunderstorm! Within minutes, the horizon swirled with thick dark clouds and I could see the fast-moving squall line racing my way.

No lunch for me today. I left for the car.

Could this really be possible? The sun was still out behind me and the storm was over the yellow field. You can see what happened next.

I could hardly believe my eyes. There was the photograph. And the caption wrote itself: "Plot of gold at the end of a rainbow!"

Let me introduce Jason and Jesiah Waldner, two Hutterite brothers living on a communal farm near Fordville, North Dakota (above).

The Hutterites, an often-persecuted Christian Anabaptist sect from Europe that fled to America's northern plains states and Canada in the 1870s, live by a very simple code. They eat, live and work together and do not own personal property. Like their Amish religious "cousins," they shun modern forms of communication (TV, radio, movies) in order to avoid the materialistic "temptations" of contemporary society.

But the Hutterites are quite at home with cars, airplanes and computers. More than 36,000 Hutterites live on U.S. and Canadian communal farms.

Three-year-old Lois enjoys a romp along the North Dakota prairie (right) while her brothers Jason and Jesiah pitch supper to the hogs.

Spend just a few months traveling the back roads of America, and you'll soon discover that the fire of religion burns brightly – from a small town in Connecticut to the islands of Hawaii and almost everywhere in between.

In Ballinger, Texas, I met a man who'd been called to erect a 190-foot cross beside an interstate. Steve Thomas (right) followed his dream, and the cross soon became the stuff of legend for miles around. Steve told me he might have raised this familiar symbol of Christianity even higher. . . but the Federal Aviation Administration requires a blinking warning light for airplanes on any structure taller than 199 feet.

He didn't seem offended by the fact that his monument was subject to a federal regulatory agency. It took 40 years to build the world-renowned Mormon Temple in Salt Lake City, Utah, but the long wait was apparently worth it. More than 6 million visitors trek to Salt Lake City each year to marvel at

the awesome headquarters of the Church of Jesus Christ of Latter Day Saints.

I shot this photograph of the Temple at sunset (above), with the help of a "poor man's helicopter"– a high-rise window ledge across the street.

Wandering along a two-lane blacktop in rural Colorado, I found a man who may have the most scenic job in all of America (following pages).

Framed by the breathtaking, snowcapped summit of 12,721–foot Mount Peale, he spends his days sawing and milling logs for his busy Rocky Mountain Lumber Company.

When he asked me why I had stopped to take his photograph for a book on America, I just nodded toward the mountain.

He paused for a moment and turned off his chainsaw. I could see he understood.

Ever wonder just how wide open the "wide open spaces" of Montana really are?

Two statistics from the U.S. Census Bureau tell the story in black and white. They show that in the U.S. as a whole, 79.6 people inhabit each square mile of the landscape, on average. But in free-ranging Montana, an average of only 6.2 people live on each square mile.

Conclusion: Montana's 904,433 residents named their state correctly when they decided to call it "Big Sky Country."

Blessed with snow-dusted mountains, crystal rivers and vast tracts of rolling forestland, Montana provides a haven for people in search of breathing room.

This couple runs an isolated sheep ranch miles from the nearest town and they insist on performing most of their daily chores the old-fashioned way. In their bucolic world, mowing thistles (previous pages) is best accomplished with the help of a couple of graceful Belgian workhorses.

They live in a wooden cabin and heat it with logs cut from their own thousand-acre patch of Montana. After a day of hard work, they also bathe in their own crystal-clear spring (left), just a few steps from the homestead.

Refreshing? Idyllic? No wonder they like it out here.

Idling along a back road between Albuquerque and Santa Fe, New Mexico, I drove past a house garnished with bright red peppers.

But why? Was this some sort of Hispanic-American religious ritual? Were the red-hot chiles intended to drive off pepper-fearing evil spirits?

It was time for some old-fashioned reporting.

Using what I could remember of my high school Spanish, I did a bit of interviewing and a secret was soon revealed. In New Mexico, thousands of farmers grow peppers during the summer and pick them in the fall. Then they dangle the colorful pods on strings (called *ristras*) attached to their roofs. After a few weeks of drying outdoors, explained the helpful Mexican-American farmer in the window (right), the peppers are ready for their role as a key ingredient in Mexican-American cooking.

Muy caliente!

Across the border in Colorado, Mother Nature turns the thermostat down, way down, by early December. The results are often unpredictable. This abstract ice sculpture (following pages) transformed a goat-pen fence into a work of art early one morning – after a local farmer left his sprinkler running all night.

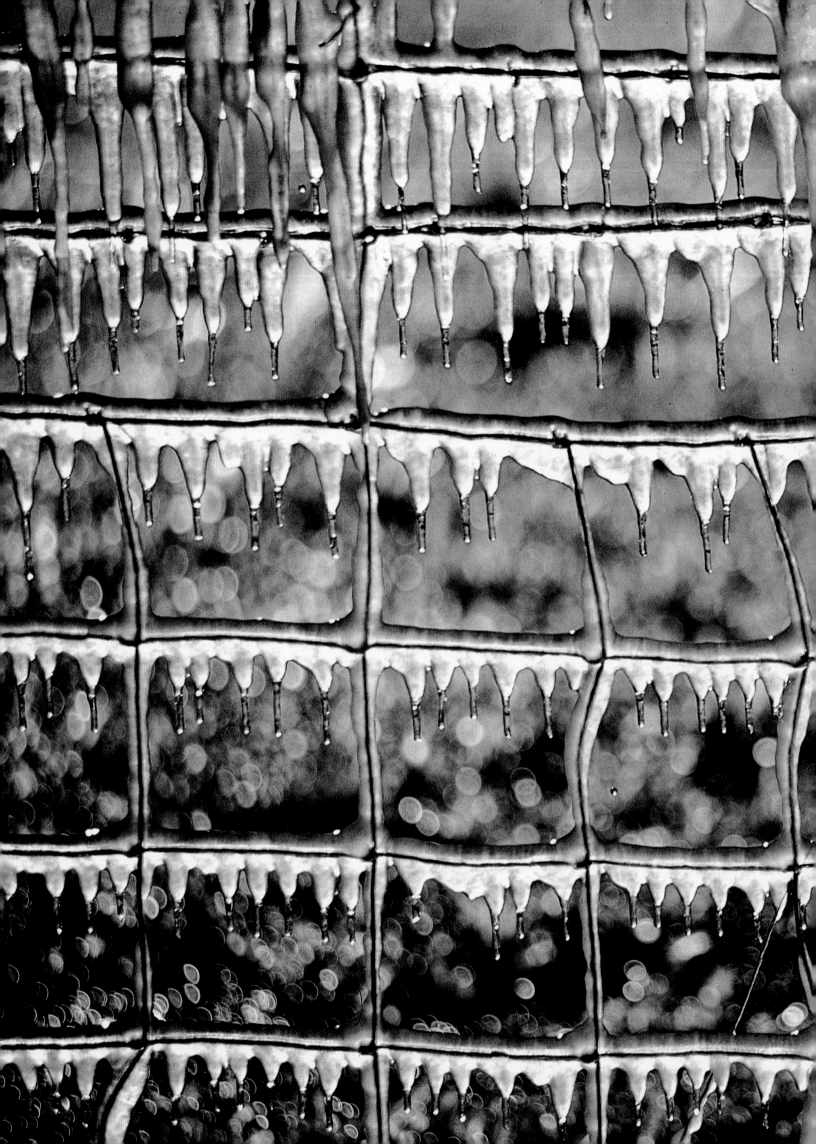

It happens every August in an otherwise sleepy South Dakota town of about 5,000.

The name of the town: Sturgis. The name of the event: Black Hills Motorcycle Rally.

For seven days, Sturgis plays host to more than 450,000 motorcycle-worshipping fanatics from all across the nation. Most of the riders thunder into town aboard clattering, chrome-plated Harley-Davidson "Hogs" – and some of these high-powered machines cost upwards of $50,000.

Bikers spend the high-octane week attending motorcycle races, parading the Hogs up and down the streets. . . and also paying $2 and $3 for the privilege of smashing foreign motorcycles (think "Kawasaki" and "Honda") to smithereens with sledgehammers.

At Sturgis, you're likely to see anything. This rider arrived on a Harley covered with a buffalo skin that included the bison's head and horns (above).

In places like this, you always ask permission before pointing a camera.   One proud biker-dad was only too happy to oblige – provided he could include his son (right) in the portrait. Along with his wife, they'd just biked to Sturgis from Leavenworth, Kansas (some 700 miles across the Great Plains), and the tot was understandably pooped.

302

Right around the corner from a notorious Colorado outlaw hide-out, "The Hole in the Wall," this old-fashioned "general store" (left) looked as if it hadn't changed since 1900. (That was the year when Butch Cassidy and The Sundance Kid slipped out of The Hole to gain national notoriety with a daring daylight robbery of the Bank of

Winnemucca, Nevada, in a front-page heist that netted their gang $32,000.)

In El Paso, Texas, I came upon another timeless scene: a Mexican boy waiting patiently outside a grocery store (above) while his mother shopped for boles, salsa and other traditional Mexican-American staples.

303

A skier zooms down a steep slope at the famed Telluride Resort in Colorado – and he makes it look easy (right).

If only things had gone so smoothly for the photographer!

What I didn't anticipate, as I skidded down the mountainside, was the impact of high altitude on human physiology.

At 13,000 feet, the air gets mighty thin. And when you've spent most of your life in Delaware (I live maybe 20 feet above sea level), the air feels even thinner.

Getting down the slope wasn't too bad – but when I started back up with my cameras and other gear, it felt like a giant's

hand was wrapping around my lungs and squeezing. It took me nearly half an hour to climb just 300 yards, wheezing and gasping on every step.

Telluride posed a formidable challenge, but photographing a group of bungee jumpers (above) in Idaho required both physical stamina and nerves of steel. To get into position, I rappelled down from a railroad bridge and tied off 300 feet above Bitch Creek. Fitting name, I told myself as I dangled there waiting for the bungee jumpers to take their turns. Why did they take so long to make their leaps? (But then again, I wasn't jumping off the bridge with my life depending on some rubber bands tied to my ankles.)

From the Here's Something You Don't See Every Day Department: A wedding reception in a pool hall!

While drifting around Minneapolis, Minnesota, on a summer afternoon, I met a bride and groom who were savoring a bottle of champagne at an outdoor café. Within a few minutes, they'd invited me to their wedding reception (left) at a pool hall across the Mississippi River in St. Paul. Yes, the bride cut the wedding cake and tossed the bouquet. But the *real* fun began when the newlyweds got down to some serious eight-ball.

In Superior, Nebraska (pop. 2,060), local artist Ann Beeson (following pages) creates her own "picture show" on the wall of a downtown movie theater. The blue tones along this traditional-looking American main street were supplied by Mother Nature, where I found the artist working on her mural by gaslight in the pre-dawn quiet of a new day.

So how does a town wind up calling itself "Superior?"

In this case, it wasn't civic vanity. The name was actually chosen by 19th–century settlers impressed with the "superior quality" of farmland along the nearby Republican River Valley.

What can you say about an American city of one million (previous pages) that includes among its attractions an imitation volcano ("eruptions" every hour on the hour), a soaring glass "Egyptian" pyramid (Luxor meets the Mojave!) and scores of human beings who appear to be sequin-studded reincarnations of dearly departed Elvis Presley? Plus 13 of the 15 largest hotels on Planet Earth?

Most visitors say something like "Wow, look at that!" as they cruise The Strip (a.k.a "Glitter Gulch"). Many writers have tried to capture the spirit of this 24-hour-a-day "Sin City," but it's not easy to word-paint a landscape that contains a faux Statue of Liberty parked beside an imitation medieval castle and right up the street from Nevada's own version of the Eiffel Tower.

The casinos also defy description. They run 24 hours a day, and you won't find any clocks or windows inside these seething hives of gambling ecstasy and desperation.

So what does it all mean? I can't begin to tell you. That's another book.

The rock 'n' roll era of the '50s and '60s returns to Reno with vengeance during the annual "Hot August Nights" (right). Thousands of hot rod and old-car buffs from across the country cruise around town in their ancient DeSotos and Studebakers, and drag races are legal (though carefully supervised) at what resembles the world's largest drive-in. Visitors can attend sock-hops and a prom – and everywhere you look, the scene features saddle shoes, poodle skirts and greased-back hair. Night after August night, the "Biggest Little City in the World" be-bops to the "golden oldies." And the favorite sound? Motown, of course.

America's known the world over for its continuing love affair with the automobile. Think of Henry Ford cranking out all those Model Ts during the early years of the 20th century. You could get any color you wanted – as long as it was black!

In the Civil War-era gold-rush town of Virginia City, Montana, I found one of Henry's original Model T pickups parked between two clapboard sheds (below). The buildings looked a little run-down, but the antique Ford gleamed with wax and polish.

The first production Model T Ford was assembled in 1908 and, during the next 19 years, Ford Motor Company would build 15 million automobiles with the Model T engine. But these days the U.S. auto industry manufactures 15 million cars every year, and doesn't break a sweat. Henry Ford's assembly-line operation was a key engineering breakthrough that helped shape the world we now inhabit. But what would the crusty industrialist think about the brilliant colors on today's cars?

A 1960 Corvette license plate tells you what the owner

thinks of his classic during the "Hot August Nights" antique-car festival in Reno, Nevada (left). Many Corvette buffs insist that the '60 model was the greatest car ever built.

How far will automobile-loving Americans take their passion for Cadillacs, Mercurys, Buicks and all the rest? This far: Six families near Alliance, Nebraska, astonished their neighbors back in 1987 – by capping their yearly reunion with the construction of a monument to the American automobile.

The result was "Carhenge" (following pages), an automotive duplicate of the world-famous Stonehenge Monument located on Salisbury Plain in England.

The original Stonehenge, a circular arrangement of giant stone megaliths, was reportedly designed as the centerpiece for a mysterious, long-vanished religion.

But America's auto-based "religion" is still very much with us. These days, you can cash a check, shop for groceries, go to church and even get married – all without ever climbing out from behind the wheel.

His name is "Tiny," and he runs the "Dart-Toss Game" at the Oklahoma State Fair each summer (left). You have to like any guy who tacks up a sign that says: "Kids Play 'til They Win!" Despite his guarantee, Tiny's balloon game was a little slow that afternoon. He simply faced too much competition from the midway rides, rodeo and livestock shows.

Thousands attend the pilgrimage each year (following pages). "Mass Ascension" begins at dawn when all eyes look toward the heavens and the sky lights up with hundreds upon hundreds of hot-air balloons.

This is the "Holy Grail" of hot-air ballooning. What Sturgis, South Dakota, is to Harley Hog riders (*see pages 300-301*), Albuquerque, New Mexico, is to hot-air ballooning enthusiasts. Each October, pilots and crews gather here from around the globe to gently waft on desert breezes, while showing off their riotously variegated balloon designs.

I caught a ride with one of the early-risers . . . and soon found myself looking down on about 600 hot-air bags at various stages of inflation. The pilgrimage is a Mecca for photographers, as well as balloon buffs.

Drive the 350–mile–long coast of Oregon and you'll probably find yourself leaning out the car window every few minutes: "Whoa . . . spectacular!" One state park after another has preserved the natural beauty of the rugged coastline.

Punctuated by massive outcroppings of hardened sandstone (the famed Sea Stacks), the wave-walloped coast also makes for some of the Pacific's best surfing. Here, a solitary wave rider (previous pages) carries his long board toward home at the end of another day on the water.

Farther down the coast, the Heceta Head Lighthouse (right) throws a high-beam into the gathering darkness of another foggy Pacific night. Perched on an exposed, rain–swept cliff near the exquisitely named Devil's Elbow State Park, the lighthouse soars 205 feet above the surf.

The tower was named after early Spanish explorer Don Bruno de Heceta, and it probably ranks as the most photographed structure of its kind in the entire U.S.

Not far from the lighthouse, the Sea Lion Caves (following pages) provide one of nature's more unusual displays. While the Pacific gushes in and out of the grottoes with the regularity of a heartbeat, golden Steller sea lions and their purple-hued pups lounge on the rocks.

During the summer breeding season, enormous 2,000-pound bulls arrive and patrol rock ledges flanking the caves.

The Sea Lion Caves have been described as "the Treasure of the Oregon Coast." It seems to me the Sea Stacks and the Heceta Head Lighthouse also deserve a shot at the title.

The soft light of a summer sunset transforms the Seattle skyline into a palette of twilight hues (previous pages). More than 2.5 million people now live in this rapidly growing mecca of the Pacific Northwest – where the vivid landscape often features breathtaking views of Puget Sound, the Vashon Islands and the mighty Cascade Mountain Range.

That's 14,410-foot Mount Rainier, snow-capped and looming some 68 miles in the background.

A German body-builder "flexes his pecs" in the iron-pumping capital of the world, California's Muscle Beach (left). Part of the famed Venice Beach complex of health clubs, weightlifting gyms and "body shops" that long ago became a staple of Southern California culture, Muscle Beach has produced several bodybuilding superstars who went on to international celebrity. Among the best-known: veteran health- and-fitness guru Jack LaLanne, former movie action-idol Steve "Hercules" Reeves and of course, the celebrity Governor of California, an astonishingly well-muscled, Austrian-born Republican named Arnold Schwarzenegger.

As local arts and entertainment took hold and prospered around Santa Monica, so did the city's now famous waterfront complex (following pages). Since 1909, the Santa Monica Pier has hosted concerts, swimming events, amusement rides and several of America's earliest national radio and television broadcasts. Route 66 (for decades the major east-west highway across America) ends at the foot of the pier, which long ago became a national symbol for the laid-back and sun-drenched California lifestyle. These days the pier, surrounding beach and winding ocean-front sidewalk serve as the rollerblading and surfboarding capital of Southern California. Fashion photography shoots, television shows and moviemaking also provide daily doses of celebrity glamour. Is it an accident that the world's largest fantasy factory, Hollywood, is located right up the street?

No matter where I looked, there was always something happening in San Francisco's Chinatown. Fish flopped from bucket to sidewalk while children poked at turtles swimming in a saucer. Ducks roasted and pig heads stared from countertops. Fresh fruit was picked over until there was nothing left but seeds and peels. And that was all within a single city block.

Chinatown's 16 blocks are the most densely populated in the nation, and the mob of people made shooting pictures there a challenge. As soon as something caught my eye, it changed. Or moved. Or got lost in the crowd. Luckily for me, Walter Wong (right) had plenty of ducks to hang in his window at The New Golden Daisy.

335

It's the longest-running game show in the history of television, and it's still going strong.

Launched back in 1956, "The Price Is Right" celebrated its 6,000th episode on March 1, 2004, as veteran host Bob Barker (left) triggered the usual audience choruses of "Higher!" and "Lower!" while offering contestants prizes ranging from a Cadillac to the latest high-tech computers and DVD players. Compare those prizes with the vinyl 45-RPM records and "All-Aluminum" cookware that original host Bill Cullen gave away in the early days of the show.

Taped at Hollywood's famed Studio 33, recently re-named The Bob Barker Studio, TPIR has awarded guests nearly $200 million in prizes during its 48-year run. I was there on stage the day Jennifer Brewster from Georgia won a pool table and a camper trailer, along with a trip to France in the "Showcase Showdown."

Hang-glider Greg Putnam soars over Mount Haleakala, the highest point (10,023 feet) on the Hawaiian island of Maui. He says he enjoys "catching the thermals" that rise from Haleakala, a mountain peak so high that local road signs warn motorists about the poor visibility than can be caused by "driving through clouds."

Greg had no problem with the visibility the day I met him. The lush, green mountainside blended into the cool, blue hues of the Pacific Ocean and it seemed you could see forever (following pages).

"We trade a lot of visions and dreams," Maui Loa told me as he showered (above) in front of his homespun museum in Haleiwa, Hawaii. "My ancestors traded with Cook and Vancouver." He continues their tradition of "cultural fusion," selling aboriginal art and pre-Columbian artifacts to modern discoverers of Hawaii.

Cliff diver Tony Clinton (left) moved from Florida to Hawaii to entertain tourists with plunges from as high as 60 feet at Waimea Falls.

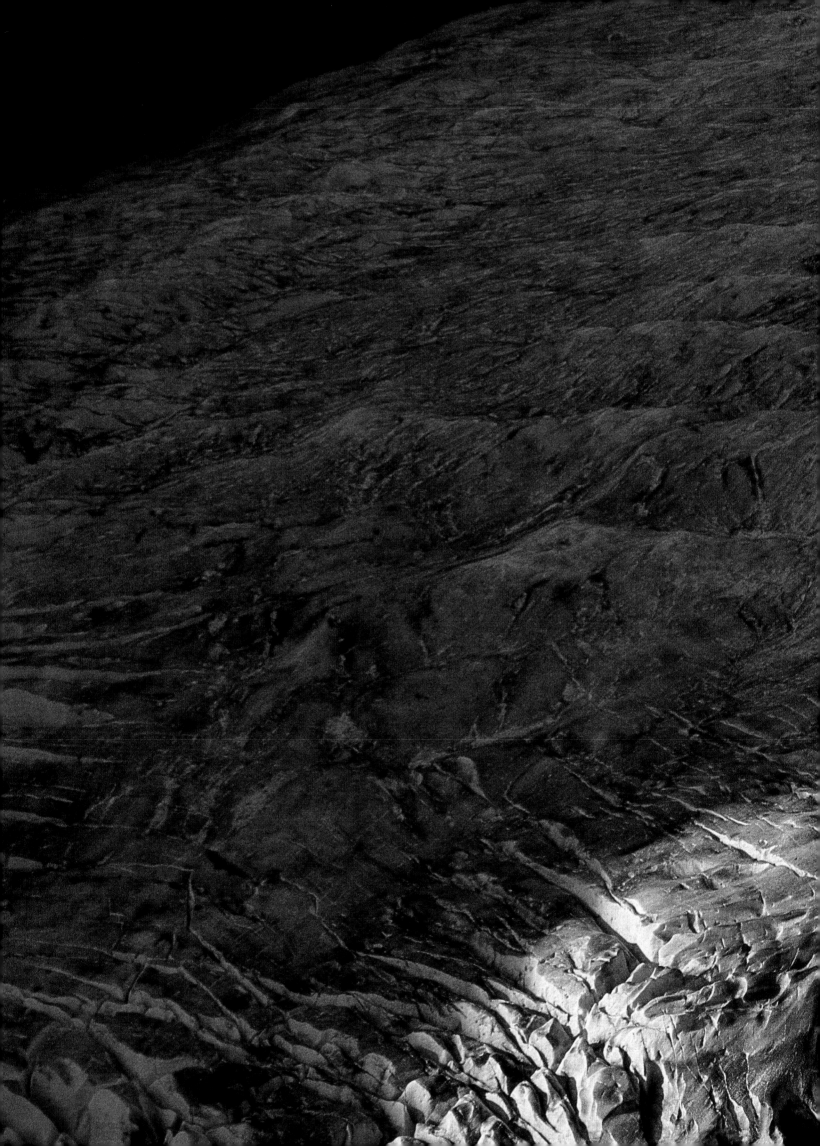

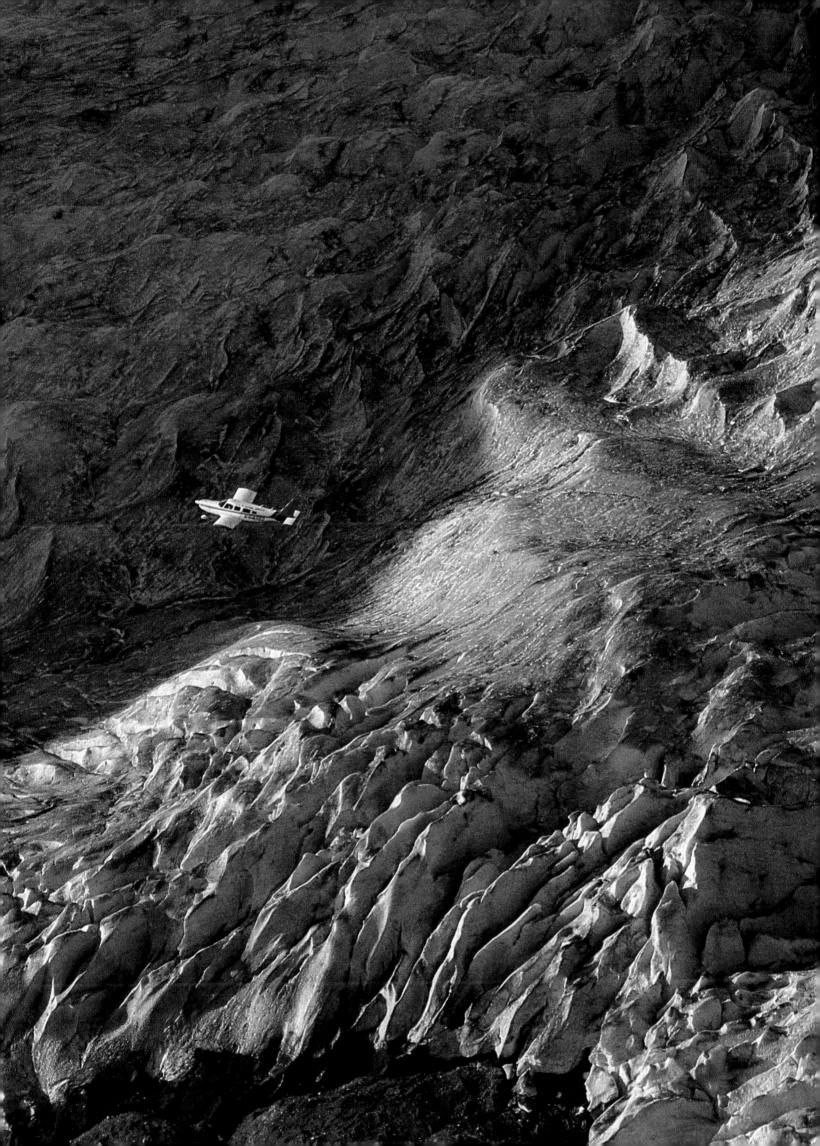

Alaska. The name comes from the Aleut language of the far north, and it means "Great Country."

Trust me: The Aleuts got it right.

Everything about America's northern-most (and westernmost) state appears gigantic to a visitor – starting with the land mass itself. With more than 365 million acres, Alaska dwarfs even Texas, which can claim only 171 million. . . making Texas less than half the size of its neighbor to the north.

And how about mountains? Sure, everybody knows that Mount McKinley ranks as the biggest mountain on the North American continent. But did you know that this monster-sized state contains 39 different mountain ranges, in addition to altitude-champ McKinley?

Like many newcomers to Alaska, I started my tour in a "floatplane" (left), while flying from one town to the next along the well-traveled "Inside Passage."

As I made my way from logging camps to wilderness areas to immense glaciers reflecting a cobalt-blue sky, I soon came to understood why Alaska's 643,786 residents proudly refer to their state as "The Last Frontier."

From a few hundred feet up, I marveled at the colossal Riggs Glacier (previous pages) – a single ice cube that stretches for more than nine miles, and stands 15 stories tall in places.

Everything seems super-sized in Alaska, and the state fair in Palmer is no exception. But it wasn't the giant 105.6-pound cabbage or enormous carrots, onions, pumpkins or flowers that caught my eye. It was four-year-old Michelle Thompson (below) and her mischievous grin riding a float in the kick-off parade. More than a quarter-million people attend the

Alaska State Fair every August. Somehow they are able to keep the affair a friendly, homegrown "old fashioned" celebration of their Matanuska Valley agrarian roots.

Anchorage, Alaska, a city of a quarter-million people (right), glows as sunset reflects in mirrored buildings and a rainbow lands in the distant Chugach mountains.

I think it rained every day I was in Ketchikan, Alaska. And every day, I watched tourists spill out of their cruise ships seeking shelter. They found it in the bars, restaurants and gift shops that lined the waterfront of this fishing and logging town. Crew members washed and painted ships (right) while their passengers roamed around town and spent money. Soon, they were called back by a blast of the ship's horn. And as quickly as they arrived, they were gone. And it was quiet again, until the next cruise ship.

Once a fish camp for Tlingit and Haida tribes, Craig, Alaska (following pages), on Prince of Wales Island has been a commercial fishing center since 1907. The salmon industry has endured many boom and bust cycles over the years and Craig (first known as Fish Egg) has flourished or struggled with the salmon runs. Drop by from April to July 4th if you want to give salmon fishing a try and you can have a shot at the title in the Craig-Klawock King Salmon Derby.

The Last Frontier includes more than 76 million acres designated as "Wildlife Refuge Areas," including the amazing Brooks Falls (following pages) in Katmai National Park. The scene here is dramatic beyond description, as spawning sockeye salmon leap frantically through the boiling spray only to be snagged in midair by brown bears and then ripped to shreds and eaten alive.

The Brooks Falls action will leave you breathless. To get back here, where the sockeyes were hatched, the salmon have fought their way across the Pacific twice, swimming as far away as the coast of Japan before returning. Driven by their inexorable reproductive instincts, they must now battle their way upstream in order to spawn – while running a gauntlet of ravenous bears. The feeding frenzy of these 1,000-pound brutes, as they take on fat for the long winter hibernation ahead, is truly an awesome thing to watch. Take my word for it: You won't find a better example of "the struggle for survival" on Planet Earth.

Alaska's fishermen know the life cycle of the salmon too. Here (right), a crew working Clarence Straight near Ketchikan, often described as "The Salmon Capital of the World," hoists a whale of a catch aboard.

Five–Second Salmon Quiz: How many of these magnificent fish does Alaska provide for the world's dining tables each year?

Answer: About 200 million.

My journey across America began at sunrise on the East Coast, just a few feet above sea level in my native Delaware, where a boy named Jeremy handed me a basket of strawberries (*pages 4 and 5*). It ended some 3,500 miles away in Alaska where I photographed Sarah Turner (left) – a girl who could pass for Jeremy's sister – and the 20,300-foot summit of Mount McKinley (following pages) at the dawning of a beautiful Alaska day.

As I watched the sunrise touch the snow-capped peaks, I considered the differences between Delaware and Alaska. The two couldn't be much farther apart. Yet many striking similarities connect them. Throughout my travels I wondered how a Maine lobsterman, a Mississippi sharecropper and a Navajo medicine man are related.

The same back roads linked everyone I met. They spend their days fishing or farming or working the same land. And they are all Americans.

Something else brought everything together.

As I searched high and low for the heart of America, through all 50 states and so many cities, I finally realized what it was.

As the dawn broke over the mountain, I understood that the same light that sparkled over Jeremy's shoulder in Delaware and glistened atop capitol domes in Annapolis and Des Moines would also brighten the new day in Alaska.

I had chased the light across the country. Sunrises and sunsets led me to places I otherwise never would have discovered. And my camera gave me a reason to stop and meet everyone along the way.

The Heart of
America
Kevin Fleming

I love the view from my office but the hours start very early most days. That's me photographing
Monument Valley, Utah. While photography is intensely personal it is also very much about sharing.
Crisscrossing America for this book I had the good fortune to meet to an incredible variety of fascinating
people and explore hundreds of spectacular places. I hope you have enjoyed the experience as well.

Portfolio Books
Post Office Box 156 • Rehoboth Beach, Delaware 19971
800.291.7600 • 302.227.4994 • info@AmericaBook.com
www.AmericaBook.com

The Heart of America Staff:

Tom Nugent	Editor
Larry Nagengast	Text editor
Jaime Anderson	Art director
Dolores Michels	Assistant editor
Nancy E. Lynch	Copy editor
Terry Plowman	Copy editor
Ken Mammarella	Proofreading
Patricia Lamb	Proofreading

Signed original prints by Kevin Fleming are available at www.AmericaBook.com or 800.291.7600
Stock photography for publication is available at www.Corbis.com
printed and bound in Italy by Mondadori • color scans by Baltimore Color Plate